OTHER PEOPLE'S CHILDREN

Foster Care Revealed

BY

LOREITA RICHARDS

Other People's Children: Foster Care Revelaed
Copyright © 2016 Loreita Richards
All rights reserved.

Cover and book design: Vladimir Verano Third Place Press

Cover image: © TW Creative, via iStockphoto

Author contact:
Authorl.richards@gmail.com

ISBN: 978-0-9982390-0-2

This book is dedicated to my family, my supportive friends and my Finn Hill girls. I love you all.

FOREWORD

ALL THE STORIES IN THIS BOOK ARE TRUE. The names have all been changed and the chronology is mixed. I did this on purpose to protect the confidential nature of the information. One story may be from 1976 and the next one from 2003, and then back to 1986, etc. I have left out identifying information regarding families. There are lots of stories I wanted to write, but I could not do so and protect the identities of the children and their families. It is not my intention to hurt anyone; it is my intention to give a glimpse into a world that has remained closed to the general public. I hope that I have given a picture of the nature of foster care, its heartbreaks and its rewards. I have criticized the system because change is needed and I hope that this may be a voice for others who spend their time caring for foster children.

I want to thank all the many people who encouraged me to write this book. I want to acknowledge all the great social workers I have worked with and to give them high praise for the impossible things they have been able to do in the service of children. I want to thank my family for their willingness to share their home and their mother with so many kids. I could not have done it without their love and support.

Some of the issues mentioned have been resolved; children now receive Orca Cards for transportation instead of bus tickets. Foster Care Rates have increased but still have not kept up with the rising cost of living. Treehouse continues to upgrade services and everyone who works with foster children is grateful for the services they provide.

OTHER
PEOPLE'S
CHILDREN

*To be owned by a wicked, corrupt system was a terrible burden I want
not to describe in this letter, but I will speak of Rita's house, the light
along the way and the things that dwelled within. She is a painter and
in every room in her house hung large oil paintings of vibrant color,
orange is her favorite. She painted portraits, abstracts, flowers, and she
had a strange and special way of depicting the relationship between
rocks and water. In the bottom of the house, where the girls slept were
several portraits of young women who had come before, giving us a sense
of history like ancient words on rock walls, making me realize I was
part of this story she has now begun to tell. When I came, Rita was no
longer young, though it would be incorrect then, or now, to call her old.
Her children were grown and I was amazed by this accomplishment
because I saw the overwhelmingly adverse conditions. Fate cast to her
that she do this alone in times even harder than now. When I lived
in her home, I was suffering from a terrible loss, unsure that I could
survive the pain. There was a black and white photograph that hung
in her bedroom of a very attractive Native-American man and also a
painting of the man in a feather headdress. I asked her who he was,
I asked many questions, and told her many things in the year-and-a-
half I lived there, but this was the story from her past that would touch
me deep forever shaping the way I feel about love, death and ghosts.
The man in the photo was the husband of her youth. She was very
beautiful then, as was he. She had a romance and three babies with
him. One night they went to sleep and in the morning when she woke,
there laid his body, but his spirit had left. I didn't think I could survive
such a thing, I love men so strong. I realized how powerful she was and
how powerful life is by this and other things Rita taught to me, that to
face this life requires one to be brave and so I learned to be a warrior.
I would watch Rita paint in the morning light at the kitchen table*

and feel the process pulling me in. I am a painter now and she deserves credit for igniting that in me. It is amazing to see a woman in action, it is best to teach by example, and she is certainly that.

In my bedroom I shared with a young pregnant woman, sleep did not always come fast at night. The room would be dark, but for the dim light shining through the cracked door from the hall, making visible the painting that hung in my room. There was a clearing in a dark forest, the night sky above a blazing fire, ghosts in the smoke, a dancing Indian with a wolf's head upon his own. The man would move as though living, the fire, the ghosts, winds in the leaves as if I were watching from the wood, lying in my state-assigned bed. In this way, I remembered who I am. It can be easy to forget who you are when you are a captive. I pray for freedom for myself and for my people. In her house, for me, hope like her fire paintings blazed and it was a crucial stop on my own underground railroad. I spoke more deeply and she listened more intently than anyone ever had. This train will keep moving. Thank you for all the fuel your love gives me, Medicine Woman.

I HAD MY FOSTER HOME LICENSE FOR ONE WEEK when my first placement came. The after hours placement operator called and said they had a 15-year-old female who had run away and she needed shelter for two days while the social worker arranged transportation back to Montana. A police officer delivered her to my home and he had no paperwork. In our classes, we had been told not to accept children without paperwork. The officer acted ticked off when I demanded some documentation on this child, but he finished his police report and left me a copy. I welcomed the teen and asked her to sit down. I got out a notebook and took down information about her physical description and personal information, and attached it to the police report.

The girl was very pretty and had unusual green eyes. They were very clear and sort of sea foam green. She was well dressed and she was wearing several pieces of turquoise jewelry. She had no other clothes with her. We talked for a while and I took her to her room and gave her a long T-shirt to sleep in. The next morning, I found the window open, the bed neatly made, the T-shirt folded on the pillow and the teen was gone. My heart dropped into my stomach. I thought, Oh No! I'm responsible for this kid and I've lost her! How did I get myself into this? I thought back to the conversation I had with my doctor and the panic I felt when he told me I had to quit my job. I was working at Ruth School as a counselor and dealing with severely disturbed youth who had been placed by the court. They were assaultive and likely to explode at any minute. It was fast-paced, challenging, and I loved it.

I had just been diagnosed with rheumatoid arthritis and the doctor felt the job was too stressful. I needed to take rest breaks every two hours, ice my joints, and take medication to control the disease. The logical step was to move my job home.

As I stood in that empty room, I wondered if I had made a giant mistake. I called my licensor, Peggy, and told her I had lost the kid. She laughed and told me to calm down and to file a police report. She reminded me that I was not running a lock up facility and I couldn't stop the kids if they chose to leave. I filed my first police report and knew I had begun a great adventure of raising other people's children.

Getting my home set up and getting licensed had gone smoothly because I already had most of the requirements for licensing. I had a first aid and CPR card, and a current TB test, and criminal history check because I was already working in a state run children's facility.

I had gotten extra beds donated and I had gone to local thrift stores for extra blankets and other linens. I stocked up on toilet paper, shampoo and toothbrushes. I thought I was ready, but quickly I realized I had a lot to learn.

By the end of the week, I had five kids, two were 13 years old, two were 15 years old and one was 17 years old. Two of the kids came with no clothes, except what they were wearing, and it became clear that I needed a clothing stock. The Department of Children's Services had a room of used clothing, so we went there and got emergency supplies and the social worker gave me a voucher for $250 to go to J.C. Penney's and buy clothes for one child.

The next day we went shopping and came home with a basic wardrobe with underwear, socks, pants and shirts and a warm sweater and PJs. The teen was so happy to show off her new clothes and the other kids told her she was a good shopper. The other kid without clothes called her social worker and asked for a voucher. Her social worker told her no.

"If you stay in placement two weeks, I'll get you one then."

I was upset because it seemed unfair. What was this kid to do for two weeks? I took the kids to register for school the next day, and the teen that had gotten new clothes let the other kid borrow her new clothes to go register. All the kids in the home let her wear something for the first few days and I began to see the sisterhood that can develop when strangers are thrown together by circumstance.

I was now cooking for eight people, three times a day and providing snacks in the evening. This required a lot of groceries. My licensor told me about the food bank that we could use at a church in the north end. Once a month they opened their doors to foster parents and we were able to get many items to help out. The stores in the area donated bricks of cheese that were close to the pull date. They had laundry soap that had been cut open by mistake by stockers. There were lots of pasta products and USDA surplus items. There was a dented can section and there were mixed vegetables and soups, etc. I filled up four boxes and felt like I had scored big time! I love to cook and this really helped. Unfortunately, this is no longer available. Stores can no longer donate items that are close to pull dates. Now they throw them away.

I went to my first mandatory meeting that same month and I met about forty other people who were foster parents. Most were doing regular or long term care and most were caring for young children. There was a speaker from The Department of Children and Family Services who spoke about lice and scoliosis. We then were divided into groups according to the age and type of license we had, and I met ten other people, two men and eight women, who were doing receiving care for teens. Seven in the group were black. I didn't think this was unusual because I lived in South

Seattle in a racially mixed neighborhood with a large black population. I was introduced to the others and made to feel welcome. The group was very supportive and I was given a phone list with everyone's name on it. I was encouraged to call and ask questions and talk about any issues I might have. Jackie, the leader of the group, was a black woman about 60 years old. She took the time to make me feel at ease. She invited me to her home the following week for a potluck lunch where the group would meet to discuss issues and share information about resources in the community. There was a lot of laughter and good humor, and Peggy, our licensor, just let people visit and share. I felt I had been accepted into a very special club. After 30 minutes or so, Peggy called us to order and began to talk about payments.

The process was complicated because each Social worker had to authorize payment for the kids she had placed in your home. You were paid for the first day of placement, but not the last day. Payment had to be authorized by a certain day, usually around the 20th of the month. This went to Olympia to be processed; an invoice was sent to us, which we had to sign and return so a check could be issued. If the social worker didn't make the deadline with her paperwork, you had to wait another month to get paid.

This is how the system was meant to work, but in fact, kids came and went throughout the month and caseworkers often forgot to authorize payment at all. So it became a bookkeeping process and checks were often late. It was sometimes 60 days after a child was placed before a dime was seen in my hand. It became clear that in order to survive in this system I had to make sure to always have enough money set aside to cover two months operating expenses, so I could manage the home. Fortunately, I had a small cash reserve when I opened the home and I was still receiving about $300 monthly from Social Security and $140 a month from the VA for survivor benefits because I had my young son to support. When I hear people say someone is doing foster care for the money, I always laugh.

I had been open for placements about two months when I got a call from Peggy. She said, "Rita, I have a special case I need to talk to you about. I have a child who needs protective custody and her whereabouts must be kept secret. It will be for two weeks and she can't go outside or make any phone calls. The police want to place her with you because you are new and your name and address are still unknown. She will be placed under a false name. She will be listed on our books as Candace Carter. Her name won't even appear in our records."

With no real thought about these strange circumstances, I agreed to take the teen. It was only later, in retrospect, I understood how naïve I really was.

Two men in suits, who identified themselves as policemen and showed me identification, brought "Candace" to my home. They gave me names and phone numbers of whom I should call in case of trouble.

Candace was 16 and pretty with a round face and large blue eyes. She had burn marks on her arms, legs and back that were healing. The officers explained that she was a witness to a murder and was being kept in detention until she could testify, but someone had tried to kill her there. I asked for more details and Candace told me that she had come across the sound by ferry to shop in Seattle and was standing in front of J.C. Penney's when two girls grabbed her and forced her into a car. She was taken to a motel, drugged and stripped of her clothing. She was raped repeatedly by many men over the next few days. She was kept barely conscious with drugs and after several days of this a man came into the room with food and clothes and a rabbit fur jacket and boots. She was told to get up and bathe and dress and eat. The man told her he had made a thousand dollars with her this week. "You are a whore and here is some money. You are my whore and you can't get away. If you try, I'll kill you." The girls who had grabbed her came into the room and they told her she would be working with them. They would teach her how to get along and they would be watching her all the time.

Candace said she was out there about six weeks. She never was left alone without someone watching her. When she didn't turn enough tricks or make enough money to satisfy her pimp, he would beat her with a wire coat hanger that he heated up with a cigarette lighter. One night, another young girl was brought into the motel and the pimp gave her two shots of something. She quit breathing shortly afterwards. The pimp made the girls carry her to a car, and they drove her out of town and dumped her body.

Candace said she was being given drugs every day, and she took them willingly now because she didn't want to think or feel anything. One day, she solicited a guy in a car and he was a cop. She was arrested and taken into custody. She told her story to the police officer and they convinced her to become a witness against the pimp. He was picked up and charged with murder. The pimp had a huge network and had put out a contract on Candace.

Candace was very compliant and never went outside or tried to use the phone. She didn't talk much to the other girls, but she played the piano a lot. She was a gifted and highly trained musician. The time went quickly and one day the two officers who had brought her to my home arrived to take her away. She went to court and was a witness for the state. The pimp was convicted and Candace was returned home. I never saw her again. About a year later I asked the social worker if she knew what happened to her. She told me that Candace had run away from home about six months after she was returned there and that she had been arrested again for prostitution.

I still think about this girl and I know that she should have been given intense therapy for post-traumatic stress and drug addiction. I don't think that ever happened. When something so horrible happens to a person, they can never return to being the person they once were. We should all be more aware of the psychological damage done by sexual abuse in all its forms. I believe that at least 75% of the kids I worked with had been victims of sexual abuse.

The general public has a negative view of foster kids. They think kids are in care because they are bad. Most of the time, kids are in care because of circumstances beyond their control. It's often because the adults who should be caring for them have failed to do so. Every story is different, and yet, I have seen the same patterns repeated again and again. Drug use and alcohol abuse by the parent is the biggest cause of children being neglected and abused. Many of the kids I cared for were born into drug addiction. These kids are born with two strikes against them. There are often effects on their brain, they may have trouble learning, and often they lack impulse control, so they fail in school. There is little family support, and at an early age they end up in the foster care system. They often have multiple placements because they are very hard to care for, and foster parents burn out, so they are moved again and again. When these kids reach their early teens, they often become drug abusers themselves because they were born addicted, and they are hooked again if they ever try drugs at all.

Sedra was not a pretty child; she was over 6 feet tall and physically very imposing. She was wearing men's work clothes that consisted of brown overalls, a plaid flannel shirt, wool socks and lace-up boots with steel toes. Her hair was dyed an ugly wine color on one side, and shaved on the other side. She had a dirty-looking bandana tied around her hair. She had safety pins in her ears for earrings. I invited Sedra and her social worker to come in and sit down; the social worker told me that Sedra needed placement for about 6 weeks while she was waiting for a placement at Job Corps.

Sedra listened politely while I told her the house rules. Then I asked her what she would like me to know about her. She replied "I'm gay and I need to know what you plan to do about that." I said, "I'm not going to do anything about it. Your sexual identity is not a concern to me unless you try to start a relationship with one of my other kids. If you do that, I'll be forced to report it and you may face charges, and you will be moved." Sedra replied, "I can live with that. I'm a twin. My twin is little and cute and she's not gay. My parents think I'm a bad influence on her and I couldn't do anything right. I ran away and I've lived on the street for 6 months. My parents don't want me to come home so I'm here." I said, "Sedra, you are welcome here if you can live by my rules and live peacefully with the group. Let's get your things out of the social worker's car and get you settled in." The social worker and I began to carry in Sedra's belongings and she whispered, "Well, that went better than I expected! Thank you for taking a chance on this one, and good luck!"

Sedra quickly became a part of the group and the other kids accepted her. I often heard them laughing and joking together. I had several kids attending the Orion Center in downtown Seattle. One of the girls mentioned that she really liked going to Orion with Sedra and I asked why. She said, "No one messes with us when we are with her." I asked her what

Sedra did, and she said, "She doesn't have to do anything. She just looks at people and they leave us alone."

Sedra had been with us about 4 weeks when she asked me to cut her hair. I cut off the ugly wine color dye and evened up the shaved area that had grown out about an inch. Her natural color was a light ash blond. Her skin no longer looked yellow, and her blue eyes became the focal point of a very attractive face. The asymmetrical cut looked high-style rather than hacked off as it had before. Sedra looked in the mirror and said, "Oh Shit!" I asked, "What's the problem?" She said, "I don't look mean anymore." I laughed and said, "Put on your bandana and your black lipstick, and I think you can pass." She tried it and agreed that would work.

Sedra had received acceptance from me and the other girls, and she had become a sweet-natured, funny young woman that we all enjoyed. About 3 weeks later, her Job Corps placement came available and she left us. We were all happy for her and sorry to see her go.

One of the things I have learned in working with teens is the more caustic the early years are, the more likely these kids are to act out as teens, even if they have had several years of stability and counseling with loving people to care for them. My theory is that when a young child, birth to five years old, experiences something, they don't have context to explain it, so the world operates on magic. If a baby cries, a bottle appears. If a toddler wants a toy, the toy appears. It's magic and to some extent the child thinks they create it all by wishing or thinking. It is not reality based. If a child is neglected or abused physically or sexually during this stage, they will act out between 13 and 16 years of age. They go into another period of magical thinking and wish fulfillment, which is a way of gaining context to explain how the world works.

The child (teen) may believe they can become a rock star, even though they can't play a musical instrument. Girls run away to Hollywood to become movie stars, though they can't act. They have a very rich fantasy life and it is often more real to them than reality. I don't see this as mental illness, but it makes a teen terribly vulnerable to all kinds of exploitation. It also makes them very hard to work with because you don't know what the currency is in their world. That's when parents or caregivers are told,

"You just don't understand. You're stupid, you don't get it." And from their point of view, we really don't! However, we can't let them push us away; that's when it's really important to have (and articulate) your family values.

Every family and caregiver should spend some time thinking about what they believe are their core values. Some of mine that I live by and teach to my family and to other people's children are:

- Tell the truth as far as you can do so without causing serious harm to another. In order for this to work, a parent or caregiver must be willing to hear the truth. You may not like what you hear, but, you can't condemn the truth teller. You can condemn the action.

- Do not steal. This is a big one for me and a hard one to convey to a foster kid who has been caught shoplifting or stealing from another kid. I make it personal. "When you steal from that store, you steal from me. You steal my time and labor that I must use to earn more money to buy the things I need and want because the price has gone up because you are a thief." At that point most kids will become incensed and deny they are a thief. But logic is hard to refute. A thief is someone who steals. You stole, so you are a thief. How does it feel be known as a thief? At that point, I will talk about having self-respect and that it's hard to respect yourself if you have to think of yourself that way.

- Live within the civil law. Most kids don't even know what that means, so it becomes a talking point to explain. Do nothing that will land you in jail. Your freedom is too important to be taken lightly. Do not give it up foolishly by doing something like assault, property damage, stealing a car, speeding or driving drunk.

- Do not do violence to yourself or others except to save your own life. Treat everyone in such a way that you can always go back tomorrow. You can disagree with anyone, but do so in such a way that there can be conversation the next time you see them.

- Don't let others provoke you to anger to the point that you will lose control of yourself. Always remember that when you lose control, someone else can decide how you will behave.

~ Respect the environment in which you live: your home, your room, your school, your world.

~ When you are given a job to do for money or other considerations, take pride in what you do.

~ No one owes you a free ride. If you want something, be willing to work for it. Anything worthwhile requires effort.

~ Your behavior affects others. Try to be a force for good in the world.

~ Respect your own body and demand that others do so. Do not share your body with anyone you do not love and who does not love you. The consequences are too profound, both to you and to your chosen partner.

~ You are a child of God and there has never been anyone on this earth like you. There will never be again. You have a right to exist and you have a responsibility to the world to use your life well.

~ You choose what your future will be by what you do today. Make your choices wisely. You will pay the prices for your choices, good and bad.

Children came and went over the next four months. Some stayed one night and some stayed for weeks. I learned more about the system and found more creative ways to make the house run smoothly. Each child was given a chore to do daily and each was also required to make her bed, pick up everything off the floor and vacuum the room before she could go out. This was very interesting because it pointed out the lack of basic self-care skills these children had. Some kids had never made a bed. They didn't know how. They didn't know how to fold clothes and put them away. They just threw their clothes on the floor and picked them up when they changed. Maybe one in five had some basic housekeeping skills. It was a teaching experience for me to help them learn these skills. We had weekly cleanup on Saturday and everyone had to participate. Chores were written on a piece of paper and drawn out on a chart. No one got their allowance or got to leave the house until every job was complete. Peer pressure worked well in this situation because everyone wanted to get their allowance and bus tickets so they could be free to hang out with friends.

The kids were required to be home for meals and to eat at the table. Many kids had never experienced this in their lives.

One child in my care was so thin, it was clear that she had suffered serious malnutrition. She was 14 and beautiful. She weighed 82 lbs. Her hair was white-blond and curly and she had perfect features and a beautiful smile. Julie had a history of long-term severe sexual abuse and though she looked about 10 years old, she was provocative in her behavior and tried to dress in such a way that she attracted male attention. This was hard for her to pull off because she was so small we had to buy her clothes in the young children's section. She commented that she had never lived anywhere someone had cooked. She said, "I always thought food just came in Styrofoam boxes." Julie was not well liked by the other kids and often was picked on, but she was a quick learner and she became very interested in the preparation of food. She also tended to be naturally neat and would often clean up after the other girls. When I took her to school to register for classes, she commented that she had never had an adult take her to school before. She had just gone and picked up the papers and brought them home to be signed by her dad. She seemed to be fascinated by how my family worked. She wanted to go to college like Lisa was doing and she wanted a family where people liked each other and no one was drunk.

When Christmas came, it was a learning experience for all of us. I bought sweaters and socks and various items of make up, etc. as gifts for the girls. The caseworkers delivered a large box of presents for the kids that had come from the Holiday Magic Program. When we opened presents on Christmas morning, one of the girl's Holiday Magic packages contained a box of Kotex, a used deodorant stick and a pair of worn out house slippers. I wonder what deranged soul thought this was an appropriate gift for a foster child! From that Christmas forward, I always checked what was in the package before it went under the tree.

Through the years, I have been so grateful for the generosity of people who have provided things for my kids at Christmas. One year a young couple gave a very high quality guitar and case for one of my kids. For the next ten years this donor wrote a check for me to shop for the kids, giving $150 dollars for each kid. I was able to buy coats, hats, gloves and things the kids really needed that I could not have provided without his help.

Julie stayed at my house through the holidays and into the spring. She grew taller and began to look like a teen. Still very fixated on boys, she came to me one day and said she was going to run away. We talked a while, and seeing that I could not talk her out of it, I told her I would help her pack. I made a list of phone numbers she could call for help, packed her some food, crackers, cookies and candy bars in her bag. I told her I never wanted her to be hungry again. She took her bag and left in a car with her boyfriend who was leaving for college in Portland. I called the police and filed the run report and notified her social worker. She was picked up two days later in the college dorm where her boyfriend went to school. I couldn't take her back because her bed had been filled and I had no openings. Julie spent the next four years running away, living on the streets and doing drugs, but every now and then she would check in. She somehow managed to complete her GED and attend cosmetology school. She got off the hard drugs (though she still smoked pot), started counseling and enrolled in college. Julie got married, had a child, got a divorce; still, she earned her AA degree and enrolled in Evergreen College to pursue her BA. She visited now and then and brought Christmas gifts for the girls in my home. She said one time that she had never had stability in her life, but in my home she saw what it should look like. Julie calls now and then to ask questions about parenting her own son.

Who knows where the ripples stop when you toss a pebble into the lake? A small act of kindness can change a life, even though you may not see it for many years. Julie is one of the reasons I keep working with kids. I know I made a difference in her life.

Having a group of six teens is fraught with potential problems and drama is the norm. The group dynamics change all the time because of the turnover. One of the greatest hazards in mixing kids from such different backgrounds and ages is the bad habits kids learn, like smoking. I made a decision after a year or two not to take 12- or 13-year-old girls. They were too vulnerable to the influence of the older kids, who were often street kids, chronic runners and drug users.

I have the option of refusing any child, and I try to be selective about the mix. If I have one child who has suicidal ideation, I won't take another one at the same time. They will feed off each other and become worse in their behaviors. If I have one child who has a history of fighting, I won't take another physically aggressive child. That's the way it should work, but in practice, sometimes we are not given the facts. In the early years this was a real problem.

I remember one child particularly. About 9 o'clock the After Hours unit called. They had a 15-year-old girl who had had a fight with her mother, and her mother was refusing to take her home. The child was crying and upset. Delivered to my house by cab, she was still crying and I tried to calm her down. When asked if she had any clothes with her, she told me she didn't have clothes because she had burned them up. Asked why, she said the voice in her head had told her to. She went into the bathroom to wash her face and after a few minutes I went to check on her. There she stood, burning her arms with a lighted cigarette. She had burn marks where she had touched the cigarette to her cheeks and forehead. I asked her to "come sit down and have some chocolate milk," and I called After-Hours. When I told them to send someone to pick up the child, they said it would be 4 hours before they could come get her. I called a friend to come over because she had a car with childproof locks, and we took her back. I called my licensor the next day, and she had a fit. She was really angry, saying this child had just been released from a mental institution. She had been in several group-care facilities that specialized in mentally ill children. She never should have been placed in a private home. I never accepted another child from that After-Hours worker.

Social workers come in all levels of competence. Some are able to do the job very well and enjoy working with the kids. They really have almost total power over the children's lives and the kids who get a good one are fortunate. There are also some workers who are less able and kids don't always get the services they need. I've had kids in my home for six months and never seen the social worker. This no longer happens because of a mandate that social workers must see the child and the foster parent once a month for a health and safety check. This is a good thing. Many helpful changes have been put in place in the last five years, but we have lost a lot of support and continue to take the brunt of the funding cuts.

One of the problems I encountered was constant, excessive wear and tear on the home. Something was always being broken. The iron got dropped. The washing machine got excessive wear and dishes were broken at a high rate. Towels got packed and taken when kids left. The state does not fund these kinds of things, and all must be worked in. One rule in my home is that nothing can be put on the walls. Kids love to put up posters and pictures of their favorite stars. Tape takes the paint off and pins leave holes. Think of 20 or 30 kids doing this every year, and you can see the problem. One child carved her boyfriend's name in my dining room table-top. She seemed surprised that I was upset about that. Foster kids have no sense of responsibility for your possessions; many come from backgrounds of extreme poverty or neglect.

I have a lot of antique furniture, having collected and restored many really nice pieces. People often comment that they are surprised at how nice my home is. They don't expect a foster home to look like that. One social worker looked around my living room and commented in a snide voice, "Well, looks like the foster care system has been pretty good to you!" I don't suffer fools gladly, but manners are not handed out with a degree, and some people are of the mindset that foster parents are unable to have anything of value. I've always been a good manager and have learned that, if you have a good eye and are willing to work at restoration, beautiful things can be created from other people's junk. As a working artist perhaps I'm more able to see potential in things.

My rules and time schedules were posted on the girls' bathroom door, so everyone would know what was expected and things would be as predictable as possible.

My daughter, Lisa, was a great help; I don't think I could have done it without her. She was young enough to be a confidant to the children, and old enough to be a good role model. She often worked on her college homework while the kids worked on theirs. She had her own car – a hot-looking little Mustang II, and the kids looked up to her.

I think my son, Jason, felt the biggest impact of having the girls in my home. He was ten when I started and the only male in the house. He had some health problems that caused him to miss a lot of school and he had a learning disability. He had visual perceptual disorder, which is not dyslexia, but similar in its effect. He could read well, but he struggled with numbers. He could not copy down a number sequence without transposing the numbers. I wonder if I could have helped him more, or less, if I had not been working with the girls and instead was working outside the home. He had lots of friends in the neighborhood and liked to ride his bike and trek through the woods behind our house. There was a small stream there and he "panned for gold" and generally had a lot of time for play.

One of the disadvantages I've observed in working with disturbed kids is they seldom had a chance for unstructured playtime. Life was too unpredictable for that to happen, preventing development of imagination and coping skills. Every kid should have a chance to build a fort and make a rocket ship out of a cardboard box and pan for gold in a stream. Play is serious business. It connects us to our world in a way that a video game never will. Kids playing together, whether it's building a fort or making a castle out of Legos, learn to cooperate and negotiate. They develop spatial sense and eye-hand coordination. We should pay more attention to this developmental stage.

All foster homes are terrible places for a child – no matter how kind, how loving, how good the home is or how skilled the caregiver. When a child comes into foster care it means someone who should have been there to care for that child has failed. No matter what we do as foster parents, it will never make up for the failure of the biological parent to be there to provide a loving home. We can love, nurture, educate and support and help that child to grow up, but we cannot replace the biological parents. At some point in that child's life they will have to deal with the failure of that most essential, most sacred bond. This is why so many foster kids have a poor self-image. They feel that they weren't good enough for the parent to "give up drugs or alcohol" for them. I recently heard a child make the comment, "Drugs must be something special, my parents gave me up for them." A child will forgive a parent almost anything. A foster parent must never criticize a birth parent or disrespect them in any way. To do so is devastating to the child. You may hear horror stories, and your instinct will be to rail against the actions of an abusive parent. I've learned to say, "I'm sorry that happened to you." That's a neutral statement and doesn't assign blame. It doesn't forgive or excuse either.

I continued going to the monthly meetings and getting to know other caregivers of teens. I felt a lot of support from the Interim Care Office. Peggy and Marge were both very knowledgeable and supportive of the teen homes. As I became closer to the other caregivers, we formed a group that met in the homes once a month. It was usually a potluck luncheon; we shared some really good food, some war stories and information about community resources. This really helped to combat the feeling of isolation that can develop when you work alone in your own home. We all had phone lists and addresses of the homes in King County and the age group each person worked with. We no longer have this; I think the department doesn't want us talking to each other.

Dear Nana Lisa and Josh,

Each and every year you have somehow touched my life. I am so grateful to have had you there in my time of need and times of joys. Thank you so much.

Love, J.

AFTER FOUR YEARS OF DOING IN-HOME CARE, I QUIT. Nothing precipitated this except my son's age. He had reached 14 and I felt he needed some time to go through puberty without the influence of living with six teen girls who were often into risky behaviors. When I called Peggy up and told her I was quitting and had already accepted another position, she was shocked and angry. She came out to my home the next day and apologized for her reaction. She asked if I would keep the girls I had for 30 days. That would give the social workers time to find new placements. I agreed to do so and we parted on good terms.

My arthritis had gone into a remission and I felt that I could manage a public job. The YMCA had received the contract for a new program that was being developed. It was to be an intensive program called a Crisis Residential Center with a "no decline policy." It was to be "staff secure", which meant it would have a staff ratio of 1:2, one staff person for every two youth. The intent of the contract was quick intervention and return to home. This quickly got lost in the reality of what was a desperate need: a place for really tough, behaviorally disturbed youth. There was no place in the system serving this population. A change in the Juvenile Justice Code had made it much harder to lock kids up in Washington State, so a lot of kids who once were detained were now released back in the community. No one wanted them, no one would take them, but our contract said we could not decline any youth if we had an available bed.

The CRC facility housed 12 kids. Each had a small private room about 7 feet wide and 12 feet long. All the doors had locks, so kids could lock their room when they left them, but only staff had keys to open the doors to let them back in. The windows had heavy wire on them and the glass could be opened only about 3 inches. Each room contained a twin bed on a metal frame and one small 3-drawer chest. There was a large communal dining room, a recreational room and two industrial-type bathrooms with six showers and six toilets in each. The front area contained offices for the director, his administrative assistant and two social workers, and a counseling room for family meetings. There was also a time out room, which had nothing in it except mats on the floor. This room had bars on the window. The kitchen was on the other side of the building and the food prepared there was brought to the unit on large steel carts. We had use of a gym for basketball and a running track, as well as a swimming pool in the basement and an art room on the 7th floor.

The YMCA had many other programs and activities within the building, requiring us to move the CRC youths past offices and private citizens to go to school on the 6th floor, to swim, to use the gym, etc.

During the six weeks the program had been up and running, two directors had been hired, and both had quit. The third director lasted about four months and then Ed was hired. Ed was ideally suited for the job. He had been a troubled teen, been convicted of a crime and sent to prison. He finished his high school degree, got a college degree and came out to work with street kids. He knew the population. He was dynamic and practical.

There were daily fights resulting in two or three restraints a day. These kids were hard core! Slowly, by trial and error, we developed a strong and workable program. Everything was controlled by the clock. The kids knew exactly what should be happening at any point in the day. We developed a level system and a privilege system based on behavior. Intensive staff training included techniques in positive restraint by a team from a mental institution in Oregon. Dr. Ted Teather (my personal hero) did extensive work with us in de-escalation and behavior modification techniques. CRC was meant to be a two week program, but the kids we had were not accepted at, or had blown out of, most available state resources, so they stayed until we could find a place for them. We had become a de facto group home. After a few months, I accepted the position of Staff Supervisor. The kids were making progress and the staff was getting increasingly skilled.

The evening Supervisor was a young black man from New York named Owuor. Athletic and high energy, he had the best instincts with kids I have ever seen. He could spot trouble brewing before any of us had a clue, and could defuse a kid with a touch on the shoulder or a quiet remark. Merry Lee, the Administrative Assistant, kept everything running. She had a smile and a quiet sense of humor. Kathy, one of the social workers, was a tall blond with a quiet voice and a slow manner of speech. She was unflappable, and the kids trusted her. The line staff was made up mostly of young mean and women who had just graduated from college and were in their first positions in the social services field. Many of them would go on to become social workers and administrators in the state system. The Y program was a great training ground.

One of the kids in the program was a young man named Joel. He was almost 17, with several assault charges in his history. He was handsome, personable and articulate. He was my first primary kid. That meant it was up to me to assess his problem, develop a case plan and make it work.

Talking to Joel about his background, I found that he had been raised by his father. Mom had left when he was ten due to severe domestic abuse. Joel's excuse for his behavior was that, when he got mad, he just lost control and before he knew it, he had hit someone. Asked if he really wanted to change his behavior, he said he did because he knew if he didn't he would end up in jail for a long time. I told him any behavior could be changed if you really figure out what happens and intervene before you get to the actual behavior you want to change. He didn't believe it, but was willing to work with me. Together, we made a chart. I asked him to describe what happens before he hit someone. He said, "I don't know. I just see red and then I double up my fist and hit. It's so quick." We practiced different things that might make him mad, making only one change. Instead of making a fist, he was to extend his fingers as far as he could. We placed tape around the middle knuckle of his index fingers so that it was hard to bend them. I asked him to meet with me every day to talk about how many times he had felt angry and how he had dealt with it. He was encouraged to say "I'm feeling angry and I need to take a break." He made the changes rapidly and with a great sense of pride. For the first time he saw that he really did have control. We were able to secure a placement for him in a program that taught building trades and he left the program. He returned two years later at Christmas and told us he had completed the program and was a heavy equipment operator. He said he had never hit anyone after leaving the program at the YMCA, and now he had too much to lose to ever do that again.

Not all our kids did that well. One kid was actually schizophrenic. Jack lived on the street, and every once in a while he would turn himself in for placement. He would stay just long enough to get a hot meal, a bath and a change of clothes. He could not stand to be touched.

He watched me several times cutting hair for the residents and one day he asked me if I could cut his hair. It was shoulder length and very unkempt. He was trembling with anxiety. I spoke to him quietly, "Jack, I know this is hard for you. I'll try it, but if you want me to stop or take a break, just raise your hand and say 'break'." I began to cut his hair and his trembling grew worse. After about 5 minutes, he raised his hand and whispered, "break." I stopped and sat down about 5 feet away and said "we can start again when you are ready." After a few minutes, he whispered, "again." I finished his haircut and he said, "Okay," and left the shelter.

He came back after about three months for another hair cut and a bath. I heard, about two years later, that he had killed someone in Oregon while robbing a convenience store. He is doing "life without parole."

We got a lot of kids who were mentally ill. One young man had multiple personalities and believed he could talk to aliens. He carried an earpiece and said, "Earth to Zarco, Earth to Zarco," constantly. At night, we could hear lots of distinctly different voices in his room, and it really sounded like several people were in there having a conversation. It was so real the night staff often went into his room to check who was in there with him. It was pretty creepy.

Assaults against staff happened occasionally and certain staff people were hit again and again. This was usually because they did not use proper procedures in dealing with violent kids, or they were afraid. These kids could sense the fear and things could get ugly quickly.

I had only one incident where a kid tried to hurt me. I got bitten. We had a young girl who had tried to kill herself several times, and I was taking her to the art room on the 7th floor when she spotted on open window. She made a mad dash for the window and jumped. I caught her by the feet as she was going over the ledge. I pulled her back inside and she bit my arm just above the elbow. I grabbed her nose and held it to block her airflow, so she had to let go with her teeth to breathe. By that time, two other staff people were there to assist me. We got her back into the unit and into the time out room. I had to go to the hospital to have my arm treated. I was given a shot and antibiotics to take for a week. The girl was transferred to Western State Hospital the following day. Six months later, she hung herself at the hospital.

I tried to teach my staff about de-escalation techniques. Some picked them up quickly; some did not. Rule number one is: never block the doorway; always give the person a way to leave the room. The fight or flight instinct is very strong. Flight is always the better choice for the kid. Back up out of reach, try to maintain 5 feet or more between you and the kid, maintain a loose relaxed posture. This will allow you to move quickly if you have to, but is not threatening. Use choice statements: "I see you are really upset, would you like to talk about it now or do you need a little break?" Or, "would you like to talk with someone else?" Telling a kid, "You need to calm down," is pointless and usually makes them angrier. Saying, "I need a little help in figuring out what is wrong here," does not place blame and is a more neutral statement.

If the kid is yelling, you should whisper. Most of the time, the kid will quiet down just to hear what you are saying. Do not ever try to hug or pat or comfort an angry person. To do so brings you into their range and if they interpret your gesture as hostile, you will be hit. Give them something physical to do. "Would you like to take a walk and we can discuss this?" This changes the focus and helps them dissipate some of the adrenaline. Never, never, never tell an angry kid he or she is acting stupid or is out of control. If you tell them that, they will act on it!

Sometimes you just know from a gut level what to do. One young man on the unit had a long history of violent behavior. Dale was from Louisiana and had spent most of his teen years in group homes. He was turning 18 in 30 days and he was scared about his future. He was about 5'8" and very muscular. He carried a small cardboard "overnight" case around almost constantly. When asked what was in it, he would say, "Books and things."

The basketball games in the gym often got very competitive and one male staff person seemed to take perverse pleasure in out-playing this kid. He would "talk trash" to the kid, "You're not so hot, face it, you're just too slow," etc. The tension between them built over several days. The talk about the situation among the kids was that Dale planned to take out the staff person during Gym that evening. The staff person fed into it; I think he really wanted an excuse to get physical with the kid. The lines had blurred and egos were on the line, it was no longer staff and resident, it was two young virile males struggling to prove dominance.

Dale went 'on pass' and came back to the unit just before dinner smelling of alcohol. He had managed to get liquor while 'on pass.' This was not hard to do. I sent the staff person to my office. I told him if he came out, I would fire him on the spot and no kid was to be allowed in the locked office with him that evening. I assigned him a lot of paperwork to do and told Dale he could not go to Gym that night because he had been drinking. I asked Laurel, the smallest female on staff, to remain behind on the unit with me. Dale went to his room as directed and promptly put his fists through the window. We could hear the glass shattering and him crying. After about 10 minutes, Laurel and I went into his room with first aid supplies and calmed him down. He was crying and he let us bandage his wounds and clean up the broken glass. I don't know why, but at that moment, I said, "Dale, open your suitcase for me." He did. It was filled with seeds: packages of carrots and broccoli and tomatoes, beans of all kinds, even flowers. I looked at the seeds and I knew I was seeing the heart of this boy. I asked him what he was going to do with all those beautiful seeds and he said, "I just want to grow things. I just want to be a farmer." The next week we found a dairy farmer in Snohomish County who was willing to give him a job. He would help with the cows and have his own room and a place where he would be allowed to plant his seeds.

Part of what I did that night was gut instinct. Part of it was cultural knowledge and part gamble. I know we took a chance going into that room, but I was betting that that young man who had been brought up in southern Louisiana would not hit or hurt a tiny little woman and someone old enough to be his mother.

The staff person was harder to fix than the kid. He said I had undermined his authority and made him look weak and now the other kids would not respect him. This did not prove to be the case though and soon everything was back to normal.

And then Rick came. We had been told to expect a new resident, but had not been told anything about him. He walked in on prosthetic legs and he was about four feet tall. His arms were foreshortened and his hands were flipper-like. He had one opposable thumb that was really a toe and one short finger on his right hand. His hair was a full puffy Afro and he had a jaw deformity that made it difficult to open his mouth fully, which created a problem with his speech. He could speak, but everything was muffled.

My heart dropped! Oh No! How could they expect us to take this kid? The other kids would eat him alive! But I was wrong.

After the intake process, Rick went into the TV Lounge, hopped up on the couch and said, "Hey guys, I'm Rick, anybody got a cigarette?" Three people pulled out one and gave him one. I think the group did not know what to make of him and by the time they figured it out, he was running the show. Rick was funny and he did not recognize any limitations. He could throw a basketball from half court and make the basket every time. He could write quite well by holding a pen between his two wrists. He could eat with his "toe hand." The only time I ever saw him ask for help was in cutting meat. He couldn't hold a knife. He also had a violent temper and when he got angry, he would throw chairs. He was very difficult to restrain, because his legs would fall off and he was so short and so strong. He loved to push all the elevator buttons and run away laughing. This was a big "No, No" because the other businesses within the YMCA building did not want their clients inconvenienced, and we did not use the elevators during the day.

On an outing to a ski resort, Rick dropped one of his legs off the ski lift. I think he did that just to see us scramble for it. We took him to Freeway Park, which has tall concrete columns of varying heights, and he managed to crawl to the top of the highest one. He could not, however, manage to get back down and we had to work really hard at getting him off that pillar.

I don't think we made one dent in Rick's behavior. He was still a prankster and just as volatile when he left as when he came. But we were all different. He changed us for the better. I will never again judge a "handicapped" person. Those with limitations often have amazing abilities. Rick had an amazing spirit and a natural gift for leadership. I hope he was able to use it in some way, but I know wherever he is, people will be touched by him.

Many of the girls who came to the Y shelter were there because they had been picked up for prostitution. At that time, there was a well-developed crime organization in the area and they ran a circuit between Portland, Oregon, Seattle and Vancouver. Young run away girls were recruited and moved between the three cities. This served the purpose of making them less visible to the police and if a kid disappeared, it took a while for anyone to notice. This was during the time when the "Green River Killer" was very active. It was a scary world for these girls. One young girl, who was just 13, had been actively working on the streets of Seattle since she was 11 years old. She was very small with dark hair and blue eyes and she had a sweet and gentle nature. We had her for about three weeks and I don't know where she went, but I often wondered what had brought that baby to the mean streets and why there was no one in her life to protect her.

I came to work one Saturday morning and the night shift supervisor told me I was in for a hard day. Two female gang members from opposing gangs had been placed the night before. They had already tried to fight each other twice the day before.

We were setting up breakfast when they started again. Two staff members grabbed each girl and separated them. This became the pattern for the whole morning. We were unable to conduct any of the normal activities and the other kids were getting restless. After the fifth restraint, I called the whole staff into the office and said, "The next time these girls go at it, put them both in the time out room and leave them alone. This has become a game for them and I'm tired of playing it. One of us is going to get hurt and this has got to stop." They all looked at me shocked and one of them said, "You can't do that." I replied, "Well, maybe not, but I'll take responsibility for what ever happens and some one will have to stand outside the door and observe just to make sure they don't kill each other. I'll take the first shift at observing."

Thirty minutes later, they were at it again and we put them in the time out room and locked them in. They yelled and screamed and cussed each other and threw a few halfhearted punches and soon they both sat down on the mats on the floor and were quiet. After a few minutes they were talking to each other in quiet voices. I left them there for two hours. They never fought again.

When the shift was over that day, the staff went next door for a cold drink and an hour of decompression. We made sick jokes and laughed too loud and had a pizza and hoped for a better day tomorrow. We recalled other bad days and retold the sick and funny stories.

The one that was retold the most – until it became a mantra so that some one only had to raise their fist and wave it for all to fall out in side splitting laughter – was about the autistic boy who was with us for a few days. He spoke only rarely and rocked a lot. He went with the group to all activities, but did not participate. One evening during swim time, he went down to the pool area. He usually just sat on the bench and rocked back and forth, but that evening he went into the bathroom and came out with a large dark log of feces in his hand. He held it over his head and said, "Look Ben, Shit Ben!" and he began to run around the pool, round and round, waving his hand and yelling "Shit Ben!" At this point, Ben faced a real dilemma because if he grabbed him on the wet concrete, he would probably injure the boy. If he threw his prize into the pool, the whole pool would be contaminated and have to be drained. Ben tried to talk to him, but that didn't work so he blew his whistle and yelled, "Everybody out of the pool." The boy got in line and proudly marched upstairs still carrying his prize. He was told to put his prize into the bathroom because it wasn't allowed on the unit and he calmly complied. When Ben left the unit that night he was heard muttering, "They don't pay me enough to do this job!"

A gifted teacher named Juliett and her assistant Chris ran the school. From 1:00 to 3:00 p.m. each day these 12 kids were expected to sit in class and do school work, and for the most part they did. This is a tribute to the skills of Juliett. She had the kids reading and writing and doing basic math. She was creative, funny and nurturing. She had the kids writing poetry and one day the subject was 'Love.' Some of the kids made Valentines and wrote the expected stuff. But one boy wrote:

"Love is soft

As a Brick!"

We were all in agreement that that won the prize. It really truly described his life and summed up the experience of these kids.

The intensity of this work created a special bond among all of us who worked there. There was real risk involved, and our safety depended on us being a tight supportive group. We covered each other's backs literally and figuratively. Romances developed between some coworkers and two marriages resulted. Both those couples are still together and I believe it's because you truly get to know the real person and there is no room for pretense in that environment. Age, race, and gender are put aside and all that matters is what you bring to the milieu: Can you cut it and will you be there when the crisis comes? Will you stand beside me?

Directors left and one social worker position turned over a lot, but a core group stayed. Line staff usually burned out in about 18 months. This is typical in this type of work. The pay is low and the work is very hard. People moved between agencies and different group homes because even after you burn out, you miss the intensity, you miss the kids and you miss knowing you are making a difference in someone's life. So after a stress break, social services-type people tend to return to the field. This happened to me. After five years in the shelter, I knew I needed to leave.

I gave notice and left to start a housekeeping service, which I turned over to my daughter to run, and I went to work doing road construction. I became the administrator for a forest service contract and found myself in the high mountains running a construction crew repairing and building roads. An interesting experience, maybe worthy of another book, but the job shut down when the snow came and remained shut down until it melted in the spring.

I returned to Seattle and to social services. I ran a program for Lutheran Social Services and worked for Ryther Child Center as an-on call worker during the winter months. In the spring, I went back to construction. About halfway through the season, I was transferred to a job in Montana, which was shut down two weeks later by the Environmental Protection Agency.

Back in Seattle, the Department of Children and Family Services hired me as a private contractor to visit foster homes and conduct a survey of their needs and complaints.

Marge, who had moved up to Peggy's old Licensor position in the Interim Care Office, asked if I would be at all interested in a new program called the family CRC (Crisis Residential Center). I could have a specialized receiving home with two beds, funded by the YMCA and administered by DSHS.

I knew I needed to do this. I was coming out of remission with the rheumatoid arthritis, and knew I needed to have surgery to remove the extra bone growth that was causing constant pain in my knees. I began looking for a house to rent, gathering up supplies and going through the licensing process again.

With a lot of help from friends, I had the home up and running again. Two beds were designated CRC beds, reserved for kids with more behavioral problems, requiring a greater level of supervision. We were also assigned some of the duties that, until then, had been considered part of the social worker's duties. Our responsibilities were: register kids in school, act as liaison between the schools and social workers, handle medical appointments, keep a behavioral log and write a transitional paper about observed behaviors when the child left our home. We were to be on-call 24 hours a day, seven days a week. My monthly retainer on each of those two beds was $450; for each of my other 3 beds it was $125. This was paid even if the beds weren't used.

During this period, however, the beds were full most of the time. Most of the CRC placements were kids with mental health issues. Many of the kids were suicidal and required constant monitoring. Some were bipolar and some had aggressive oppositional-defiant disorder. Many had drug and alcohol problems.

Misty arrived with a diagnosis of fetal alcohol effect. Identified as an Indian child from Alaska, in fact she had long blond hair, blue eyes and freckles. She was sweet and gentle, funny and very high-energy. She also had a problem with short-term memory. She desperately wanted to graduate from high school, but she was failing. She could not remember what she learned long enough to pass the tests. We started an intensive study program to help her. Every evening from 6:00 to 9:00, we went over her lessons. She would read them out loud. I would read them back to her. We would go over the questions, she would write the answers. Then she would read the questions and I would recite the answers. Back and forth we would go until she had the answers memorized. Reviewing before school the next morning, she would have forgotten about half the answers. Misty would not give up and she did manage to graduate from high school. I wish I could write that things turned out well for Misty, but they didn't. She moved in with her boyfriend and got pregnant about two years later. During a difficult pregnancy, it was discovered that Misty had a problem with her heart. The doctors said she probably would not survive another pregnancy. She had a beautiful little girl and was doing well as a mother for about two years. She started using cocaine and within weeks she was completely out of control. At that point, her boyfriend took the baby and moved in with his mother. Misty was on the street prostituting to support her drug habit.

I don't know if she ever made it out or if she is dead. When children are born drug affected, then abandoned by their mother, it seems pretty easy for them to abandon their own children. I guess it's true; you learn what you live.

Heidi had never been in foster care before she came to my house and she was scared. She had heard a lot of horror stories about the system. The caseworker brought her just before dinner, when the other kids were doing homework at the dining room table. At that time the household was very racially mixed. There was an Alaska native who was short with long black hair, one Ethiopian refugee, tall and very thin, with beautiful brown skin and delicate features. We had an Asian girl who was born in Thailand, but had been adopted by a Caucasian family. Heidi was clearly uncomfortable and nervous. She blurted out, "I've never lived with anyone who wasn't white."

She turned red from embarrassment and covered her mouth, mortified that she had actually spoken her thoughts. Everyone laughed and one of the kids said, "That's okay. We don't eat white crackers, come on over and sit down, you can help us with our homework?" A chair was pulled out and she joined the table. Soon they were laughing and joking with each other. The Ethiopian girl shared that when she came she was afraid I would beat her with my cane. That's what old people did in her country. You could see Heidi relaxing and before long they had made her a part of the group.

Sometimes when a new kid enters the household tensions flare and the longer-term kids make the new one very uncomfortable. They jockey for position, act tough and try to establish a pecking order. This happens more when the new kid acts tough or superior. You know then that trouble may be brewing.

Heidi was charming and naïve and the other kids gave her "little sister" status pretty quickly. Heidi had been raised in a fundamentalist home by rigid parents. She had been home-schooled and over controlled. Her only social contacts had been in her small church. At 16, she was a complete innocent about the ways of the world. She'd been told that girls got pregnant when men rubbed their belly buttons against a girl's belly button. She had been removed from her home because her father was starting to touch her sexually. She was uncomfortable with it, even though the father had told her it was his duty to teach her how to be a woman. She confided in a friend at church and CPS was called. Heidi was amazed at everything! The girls would laugh and tell her outlandish stories just to see her reactions. Heidi caught on quickly though, and her natural charm was a great asset. She was very advanced scholastically and I got her into a special school where she promptly met all their requirements for graduation. She entered college in the fall. She was an avid student, interested in everything.

Heidi stayed with us until she was 17½. She found herself pregnant. She was shocked and surprised. She had only had unprotected sex a couple of times with her boyfriend, who was a 26-year-old under achiever. But Heidi was sure it was true love. She went to court and got permission to marry, sure that she would "live happily ever after," but of course, it didn't happen quite like that. Heidi was driven and she continued her studies. She had a lovely baby girl. She was better off than most kids who had been in foster care because she had a grandmother who supported her while she pursued her education. She left her husband after about two years because he wouldn't work and spent his time smoking dope and viewing porno on their computer. Heidi finished school with a double BA in law enforcement and business. The last time I heard from her, she had a job with the police department and had applied for a position with the FBI.

The next six years was a period for which I would give high praise to the Department of Children and Family Services. There was a push to educate and support the care providers, and there were monthly meetings for the foster parents who worked with teens.

I developed close relationships with four remarkable women from this group. Virginia was a dark-skinned black woman with an infectious laugh and love and dedication for kids. She was a member of Rose Hill Baptist Church, and every Sunday you could find her there with whatever group of kids she happened to be working with at that time. She raised her voice in praise, and she was a force to be reckoned with in her church, in the community and in the foster care system. Virginia and I were both born in Arkansas about 20 miles apart, but we didn't meet until Seattle.

Katherine was a brown-skinned small woman from Louisiana. She was scrappy and a plain speaker. She demanded that kids get the necessary funds for hair cuts and hair straightening for the African-American kids and that the state provide duffel bags and sports bags for kids to carry their clothes in. She was a tireless advocate for all kids, and a lot of changes took place because Katherine would march into the office of whoever was currently Head Administrator of Region 4 Department of Children's Services and demand whatever changes she felt needed to be made at the time. People listened to her. She was a sharp dresser and her hair was always perfectly done, but the impression people had of Katherine had nothing to do with that. She was simply fearless and spoke her mind to anyone who could make things better for kids.

Tina and Katherine were first cousins and had grown up together, but they were very different. Tina worked with teen boys and she was firm, but gentle with them. She cooked great meals and demanded respect while being very loving. Most of her boys called her "Mom" and many of them would come back to see her on a regular basis years after they had aged out of the system.

The fourth woman, Lee, was the youngest of us. A pretty woman with black hair and a creamy complexion, she always reminded me of someone I would expect to find in a corporate office somewhere. She was businesslike and always dressed in suits. Because there was no bus service where she lived in rural King County, she drove her kids around in a van. For some kids this was a good thing. It made it much harder for them to return to the streets.

It was common for kids to bounce between homes, and we often called each other to ask questions about behaviors or what worked well with which kid. We also called each other when we had a favorite kid in need of placement and we were full. We would advocate for the kids and tell each other why we thought that kid was special. Virginia had a granddaughter who needed temporary care. She called the placement desk and told them she wanted that girl placed with me, no where else. I always felt really good about that.

Joe was a head administrator who did more to support foster parents than anyone had ever done before. He left the department for reasons of health and it was a sad day for me. I knew he could not be replaced.

There had been several lawsuits over the years and complaints about some foster homes. The state created a new department called the Department of Licensed Resources. This took licensing issues out of the control of the Department of Children's Services. People thought this would be a good thing and perhaps it is. The problem, though, is that the Department of Licensed Resources has no watch dog, and they have been known to treat some foster parents with little respect. Before DLR, I would go to training at the Rainier office, where the foster parents were mostly black. This was to be expected; the neighborhood was mostly black. Slowly, but surely, this changed and after a year or two the training was attended mostly by white people. There seemed to be a push to close most of the black homes in the Rainier Valley. Rainier Valley is a mixed neighborhood with a fairly high crime rate. I believe some young white licensor with diamonds on her hand wearing designer clothes felt that the area wasn't safe for kids, even though they were from that area.

There was one case that came to my attention. A black woman, licensed, fostered two teen girls, who had been with her long-term. She was called by a social worker and asked to foster her own two young grandchildren. The cause for their removal from her daughter's home was ongoing domestic violence. The caseworker set up visitation for the children. The mother could visit on the 1st and 3rd Saturday, the father could visit on the 2nd and 4th Saturday. This visitation went on for several weeks with no problems. Then, DLR called one day to say she was being investigated for allowing into the home a convicted person: the father of these children, who was doing authorized supervised visits. They were going to remove her long-term children and her grandchildren. She had asked for a fair hearing and I don't know if she prevailed or not, but this was the kind of thing that happened again and again.

My friend, Tina, had a similar situation develop and spent 18 months trying to get her name cleared. She had a disturbed child placed with her, a boy who had made false statements about every home he had been in. He told his caseworker that there were guns in the home and that another boy in the home was selling dope. The caseworker called the police, who came out and searched the house. No gun was found. The other boys were interviewed and all said the charges weren't true, but the kids were removed and the cause was listed as child abuse and neglect. DLR took away Tina's license, though she had been a foster parent for 16 years.

Tina requested a fair hearing before a Judge Advocate General (JAG), and it took 18 months for the hearing to take place. By then the caseworker that had made the charge was no longer with the department. The JAG found the charges to be unfounded, but Tina refused to renew her license. Her health had rapidly declined during this period, and I know the stress of those charges hanging over her was a major factor.

The saying is, if you are a foster parent, it is not whether you will face an investigation, but when. I had one about three years ago. I had a teen (17½ years old) with a drinking problem, who often used poor judgment about her companions. When she failed to show up for her 10:00 PM curfew on a Saturday night, I filed a run-away report. Two days later she turned herself in and asked to return to my home. I took her back. After about two weeks, I confronted this girl on her behavior because I had seen a marked change. She had become withdrawn and depressed and was skipping school. She told me that while she was "on the run" she had been raped. I told her we needed to call the police, but she refused. I called 911 and spoke to an operator, but was told I could not file a report for a 17-year-old, that she would have to agree to talk with the officer. I called her social worker and informed her of the situation. About a week later, I received notice that Department of Licensed Resources would be investigating me for neglect of a child. I don't know what I could have done differently. The investigating worker went to see the girl at school, who told her the same thing she told me and refused to make a report. She admitted she was drunk when it happened, and said she wouldn't file a report because her boyfriend would get kicked out of his place if she did. The person who raped her lived there also, but she would not give a name or address. Even after finding the same facts that I had given the social worker, DLR tried to make an issue of the fact that I had not written down the number of the 911 operator I had spoken with. It took five months to clear this charge.

Another time a lady called the department and said I was responsible for her granddaughter getting pregnant. The kid was pregnant when she was placed with me, and I took her to the doctor the first week she was in my home, to confirm the pregnancy. That one didn't go anywhere. I told the investigator if she pursued that one, I would quit on the spot.

These are just some of the issues foster parents face constantly. Unfortunately, after Joe left, a lot of the support that had been in place for foster parents just didn't seem very important to the next administrator. Also, in the next two years, Lee moved away and Virginia died. About 18 months later Katherine passed away and then Tina died. Of the entire group that had for so many years been there for the teens, I was the only one left. Virginia's granddaughter and adopted daughter have opened a group home in Virginia's house, which is called Miller House. I'm glad younger women are taking up the work of caring for the teens, but I miss my friends!

A child placed with me late one Friday night had turned herself in to the police saying she had run away from Montana. She seemed a little spacey, but there were no major red flags. Monday morning, I got a call from the placement desk inquiring if she was still there. I told them she was, and was told someone would be there soon to pick her up. About 30 minutes later, three police officers were at my door. They handcuffed the girl and led her away. One of the officers told me she had escaped from a detention center in Montana where she was doing time for killing her mother and father.

Another time, I agreed to take a 15-year-old girl who was picked up in a stolen car. The placement desk said she was probably a prostitute. The person she was picked up with was a known pimp. The girl came in and she was stunningly beautiful. She was about 5'11" and had long blond hair and blue eyes. She looked like a high fashion model. I talked with her a lot that weekend and she told me she had been on the streets for about a year. When I asked her why, she said her stepfather started having sex with her when she was 11 years old. She said she tried to tell her mom, but her mom said it was her fault and that she was to blame for wearing shorts when the stepfather was around. She said she hated him, so she left home. "At least this way," she said, "I get paid for it."

The pimp made bail and the girl left to meet him. Three days later, the police called me for a description of the girl, what clothing she was wearing and any details I could give them. They had found a decapitated body of a young female and they thought it was her. I never found out if it really was.

I don't want to give the impression that all the kids who came to my home were drug addicts or prostitutes. Many were kids in conflict with their parents, who were quickly returned to their families with counseling, and all went well for them. Some kids came because their caregiver had died or had been hospitalized.

I remember one young lady whose father had suffered a brain injury in a car accident. She had been his main caretaker for two years and her stepmother was making her miss school on a regular basis to "baby-sit" her father. It finally became overwhelming and she asked for help. She graduated from high school, went to work and soon met a young sailor and fell in love. She's now the wife of this young man and has two beautiful children. She just needed a little help for a little while.

The years went by quickly and the kids kept coming. The years had also brought many changes in my own family. My oldest son, Mark, got married to a lovely, intelligent woman named Celia and they had a beautiful little girl, my first grandchild. Lisa got married, but she was not so lucky in her choice of mates. Her husband was a strikingly handsome young man from a good family, but it became clear quickly that it was not a match made in heaven.

Shortly after Lisa became pregnant, it was clear the marriage had failed and Lisa moved back home. There were several attempts to work out their differences, but they were unsuccessful. Lisa went through her pregnancy at home with me and gave birth to a healthy, strong baby boy. We have co-parented this child, Joshua, for his whole life. I thank God every day for the gift of being able to raise this child. This life circumstance also reinforced my need to run the receiving home because I needed to be home with Joshua to nurture his development. Having another adult in the home also gave me a lot more flexibility in my own life. I could take a weekend off or a short vacation once in a while.

Another change was the deterioration of my youngest son's health. He was in college and racing his bicycle. He had hopes of going to the Olympics, but his body would not support the rigors of the training and his condition grew worse. The hard thing was we had no real diagnosis. It would start with hard nausea, and over days he would be unable to retain food. The nausea would progress to vomiting which nothing would stop. He would end up in the hospital with severe dehydration; even the anti-nausea drugs would not stop the vomiting. The doctors finally would give him sedating drugs to put him to sleep. There were many, many tests run and many opinions, but no one seemed to know the real reason. He was diagnosed with celiac disease and put on a gluten free diet. That helped, but did not cure the problem. Told he had H. pylori infection, he was treated with antibiotics, but still it persisted. As his condition grew worse, he was told he had "Crohn's" disease, but it was "atypical" Crohn's. Finally, the head of Gastroenterology at the University of Washington told us, "We simply don't know what this is." After 42 hospitalizations in six years, we decided to try Bastyr's Clinic, which is an alternative medicine clinic. They placed him on a rigid elimination diet with doses of L-glutamine and an herbal mixture. Slowly the regime seemed to work and he began to stabilize.

I was so grateful for Lisa's presence in the home during this period. It allowed me to leave to care for Jason as needed; she would take care of the foster home. The girls got used to the fact that I sometimes had to leave in a hurry and that I might be gone for two or three days. The amazing thing was how we all adjusted to the strain of his illness and how we functioned as a family during this time.

My licensor and many of the social workers knew the circumstances of Jason's illness and were understanding. The girls in the home also realized that I needed a little extra from them; they kept their rooms a little better and were a little less testy with each other. The kids went to school, obeyed curfew and didn't run away. It was like they decided to "give back," and they did!

Slowly Jason's condition began to improve and the hospitalizations became less frequent. He was able to begin to work part-time, gradually regaining his strength and increasing his hours. Over the last five years, his health has returned and he has had about one episode a year. He works full-time and has a very productive life. I no longer live in fear that he might die at any moment, and I feel like we have emerged from a living nightmare. We are a very close family as a result of these trials, and Jason has become a most important role model for Joshua, Lisa's son. Mark and his family moved to California where he works in the movie business. He had another daughter who is three months older than Joshua. They worked hard at getting the girls up to see me each summer so they would have a sense of extended family.

During these years, I could have stopped taking kids into my home, but I never felt the need to do that. There were always one or two kids who had been with me for a while when the crisis came, and I wanted them to have the continued sense of stability and the example of people who handled life even when it was hard.

Dearest Rita,

For fourteen years you have been my anchor in life. There is not a word to express my gratitude. Please get well, please stay well. Know that I think of you everyday and that I love you.

Love, Clairese

GENERALLY, KIDS ARE PLACED ONE AT A TIME and the ages vary, but there was one group of girls that stands out in my memory because they came at about the same time and they were all about the same age. We had been in the Finn Hill house about two years and the neighbors had gotten used to us. It was in a very upscale neighborhood, not the kind of neighborhood where people were used to foster kids. The house was big, six bedrooms, three full baths, two recreational rooms and a three-car garage. It had three stories and was built into the side slope of a steep hill. You could enter the top floor of the house by crossing a bridge that ran from the cul-de-sac to the front door. The driveway was very steep, leading to the three-car garage and a walkway to the second floor level. Another walkway led around the other side of the house to the bottom floor, which contained a workshop and playroom. The back of the house faced a very steep green belt, which was covered in trees and brambles. There were neighbors on each side, but none in back because the steep hill led down about one block to another road. This geography created a feeling of privacy. Having six kids in this setting was nice because the house was so spacious that no one felt crowded. It did, however, create some issues of security. Lisa, Josh and I lived on the top floor, where there was a huge kitchen and dining room, a living room, three bedrooms with a master suite and a deck that ran the length of the back. The second floor contained three bedrooms and a recreational room, laundry and entrance into the garage. The second floor back deck was about 15 feet off the ground, but the second floor also had an entry door and two windows that faced the front of the house and were at ground level. The house had an intercom system and a security system, which I had installed.

Betti, Lyla, Jessa & Alice were 14, all in the eighth grade, and each one was dealing with a background of abuse and abandonment. All the girls had a history of drug and alcohol use, and all suffered from very low self-esteem. All four girls were very pretty. Alice, an Indian girl from the Nooksack tribe, looked like Cindy Crawford. Betti was a petite red head with big blue eyes and white skin. Lyla was a tall girl with light brown skin, perfect features and a beautiful smile. Jessa, small Hispanic/white girl, had been sent to Washington by her mother when she was 13 to live with a father she did not know. She had long red-brown hair and dark blue-gray eyes. She was the brightest of the four with a very high IQ. She was depressed and rebellious. Betti stayed about two days and left to go to the store and didn't return. I filed a run report and figured I'd seen the last of her, but two days later she walked in the front door and said, "I got lost on my way home, can I come back?" It didn't take long to figure out that Betti had a serious problem. She could not say no to anyone or anything.

Alice was a kid that destiny meant for me to have, I guess. Two years earlier, I had gotten a call about Alice from a social worker in Colorado, who told me that the mother was selling this child to men for cocaine. She had been taken away for abuse and neglect along with two younger siblings. She was being returned to Washington State but she was 12 years old and I didn't take kids that young. Two years later I got a call about her because she had run away from her current foster home. I agreed to take her. My first impression of Alice was one of gentleness. She was polite and cooperative and wanted very much to please.

The first night she was in the house, Alice and another girl sneaked out after curfew. I found them missing when I did a late bed check. The next morning, when I went down to do wakeups, both girls were in bed, like they had been there all night. I yanked the covers off both girls and told the older girl "Joyce" to pack her clothes. I was moving her. She had sneaked out before. I told Alice, "If you want to stay in my house you will never sneak out again. Make up your mind right now. Stay and follow the rules or pack. She looked at me with big round eyes like she was scared to death and said, "I want to stay", and she did.

Betti was proud and haughty. It took a long time for her to bond with us as a family, but she bonded with the other girls rather quickly. Lyla and Betti had a lot in common. They had beautiful voices and they loved to sing together. Both had very ineffectual mothers and had witnessed their mothers being abused by domestic partners.

Jessa just wanted to go home to her mother in Texas. She felt totally abandoned, and I knew she was at high risk for another suicide attempt. She wrote in her journal almost every day and she would fill pages of it with the statement, "Go Home or Die."

The eighth grade at Finn Hill Jr. High had their hands full that year. The first call came saying that I needed to pick up Betti and Lyla because they were drunk at school. It was a great puzzle to me how kids could leave the house at 8:00 AM, get to school on time and be drunk at school by 9:30. These girls were resourceful to say the least. Bit by bit the story came out as they spoke with the school counselor and me. They had stopped to pick up another kid whose parents weren't home, all decided to have a drink, and that was so much fun they decided to fill up a thermos bottle and take it to school. The girls met in the bathroom between classes and had a shot or two, but of course they were acting very strangely in English class. When the teacher got close she could smell the booze. Busted! They were suspended for three days and told that the next time they came to school with alcohol they would be expelled.

About a week later I got a call from the school to come to pick up Lyla and Alice because of their inappropriate attire. I arrived in the counselor's office to find Alice and Lyla with brightly colored condoms tied in their hair and in the shoelaces of their tennis shoes. Where the condoms came from was no mystery. We had hosted an AIDS training at our home the night before and the public health nurse who gave the training had left a basket of 100 condoms for the girl's bathroom. The idea was that if the girls had access to condoms they would be more likely to use them. I'm quite sure the public health nurse did not imagine just how they would use them. I asked the girls, "What in the world were you thinking?" Lyla replied, "I don't know what the big deal is. It was just a fashion statement!" My question to her was, "Exactly what statement were you trying for? I'm ready for sex any time, any place, any where?" They both hung their heads and looked a little embarrassed. They apologized for their error in judgment and I took them home for a one-day suspension.

Each of the girls had special issues and we set up goals to address each one of them. Betti had to learn to say, "No!" We actually set up role-play situations where she could practice saying no. We also got her involved in Alcoholics Anonymous, but that put her in contact with a lot of older men who had rather poor boundaries. Soon she had half a dozen men, all over 30, calling to offer her rides to meetings. After several conferences with her social worker it was agreed that Betti needed in-patient treatment. She went into Ryther Child Center's drug and alcohol program and started to learn the skills necessary to stay clean and sober. One of the conditions of the program was family support, but Betti's birth mother refused to participate in the program. I agreed I to act as Betti's family, and I attended the family support meetings twice weekly all the time Betti was in the program at Ryther. She often had difficulty with other residents in the house at Ryther because she felt picked on and believed that other kids weren't being honest about their drug use. She began her 12-step program and was completely focused on trying to master the steps. She began to learn the art of confronting her own and other people's behavior. Soon Betti was saying no to everything. It was sometimes hard to deal with, but we knew it was real growth on her part.

When Betti first came to our house, she was one of the most promiscuous kids I'd ever had. She would have sex with anyone who was even mildly interested and felt no guilt or sense of shame about her behavior. I knew that three different men had sexually abused her at a young age and that was the root of this behavior. Betti was born with a severe birth defect. She had a giant cyst on her pancreas and her intestinal tract was on the outside of her body. She spent months in the hospital as an infant and had several reconstructive surgeries. I'm sure this contributed to her mother's lack of bonding with her, but I determined, after meeting her mom, that she was totally unable to cope with her own life and really had nothing to give to her daughter. Betti's life had been one of total disorder. She did not know the most basic housekeeping skills and had to be taught to make her bed and how to clean the bathroom. When she did laundry, she would just throw the clean clothes on the floor. She had a system – dirty clothes on the right side, clean clothes on the left. She actually was able to dress and look good and she bathed regularly, but it took weeks to get her to put her clothes in the dresser and hang things in the closet. We finally had to use peer pressure; "No one leaves the house until all the bedrooms are clean." The other girls would clean their rooms and then descend on Betti's room and force her to get to work and clean it.

The biggest weapon we had in the clean room wars was the telephone. At that time, none of the kids had cell phones, and their whole social life depended on the phone. The girls had their own phone line and it was their lifeline. When the phone was taken away, all social life stopped. I unplugged the phone each night at 9:00 and they could have it back each morning if everyone was obeying the rules. Each kid figured out quickly that getting the phone taken away was not a good thing.

If any kid came home drunk or stoned, the phone was taken for two days and the offender was grounded for a week. They could earn back time by doing work hours. Two hours of work for every day of grounding. A week equaled 14 hours of work. I chose the work. It was not easy. It consisted of weeding or wall washing or carpet cleaning and window washing, etc. It had to pass inspection or no credit was given. Betti did a lot of work. As she grew stronger in her recovery, Betti became less and less sexually active. She also became more playful and seemed in many ways to become younger. It was like she was going back and picking up some of the childhood she had missed. She began to work harder in school and her grades improved.

The last Christmas that the four girls were together was really special. We bought Karaoke machines for Betti and Lyla, and Jessa was given a beautiful guitar by the Holiday Magic program. Alice seemed to have no musical talent at all but she made a good audience. The girls sang and harmonized, wrote lyrics and performed in the garage for hours at a time. They were actually pretty good.

Lyla was the first of the girls to go. She had found a young woman with two kids who was interested in becoming a foster parent. She was a mixed-race black woman and Lyla convinced her to take Lyla and her two brothers into her home. This woman had very good intentions, but both Lyla's brothers had long histories of criminal behavior and needed a lot of structure. Lyla wanted to change her mind at the last minute and stay, but by then her brothers had already been placed there and she felt responsible for them. Also, I think Lyla really wanted to feel more a part of the black community. The placement lasted about a year. By then both of Lyla's brothers were incarcerated for car theft and assault. Lyla ran away and moved in with a boyfriend. She managed to graduate from high school and got a job with one of the small DotCom companies in Bellevue. Her boyfriend was somewhat controlling and abusive and she left him. Shortly afterward she married a man who had two kids. Lyla got pregnant and had a little girl and she continued to work. She also began to work in a local dance club on weekends. She said she did it because she needed the money. By now she was supporting everyone in the house, as her husband seemed unable to hold a job.

One day, Lyla had reached her limit. She went home, packed her things, took her little girl and left town. I didn't hear from her for two years.

Alice went to Job Corps, where she completed high school and trained to be a dental assistant. She met a young man there and began a relationship. After becominge pregnant, she decided to have an abortion. She left Job Corps without completing the training, then went to work at a Pizza Hut restaurant. She became involved with her store manager and soon moved in with him. A biotech student at the University of Washington, he was from a family of educators, father a college professor and mother a master teacher. They were Mormons from Las Vegas and they were not pleased! They felt that Alice was not in any way suitable for their son and they offered her $5,000 to leave. I think if she had been white, they might have at least tried to accept her, but the idea of an Indian girl who grew up in foster care was out of the question.

The two young lovers managed to stay together for almost a year in spite of parental disapproval. Alice got pregnant and the boy insisted she get an abortion. He told her he could never take an Indian child home to his parents and they would disown him if they got married. Alice was brokenhearted, but she decided to have the abortion and shortly afterward he returned to Las Vegas. He did help her to get her own apartment before he left. Alice went through a long period of depression but eventually her sweet nature returned. She is now married to a man who really loves her and has two beautiful daughters. They still come home for Thanksgiving and Christmas and she calls regularly to ask questions about parenting her girls.

Jessa did well in school until the last semester of the ninth grade. She started smoking pot regularly and gave up hope of her mother ever letting her come home. Depression was a constant in her life and her counselor recommended meds, but Jessa refused. One Saturday morning, she and a friend from school went to the University District to shop. Her friend came home and Jessa didn't. I filed a runaway report and was really worried because of Jessa's depression. After much talking with the friend, she told me that they had gone to meet some guy that Jessa knew to score some weed. She said when they got there the guy didn't have any, but he said he was waiting for a delivery and it was being dropped off at a friend's house in south Seattle. He took their money and Jessa decided to go with him to pick up the dope. The friend said she was scared and decided not to go.

Ten days later I got a call from the police. They had Jessa in custody and were taking her to the hospital. A teenage boy whose mother managed a motel had called the police and reported that he had heard a girl crying and begging to be let go. He thought she was being held against her will. They raided the place and found Jessa. She had been forced into prostitution.

Jessa went from Harborview Hospital to a group home. She would call me regularly. She told about her terrible panic attacks, that they were so awful she was afraid she was going to die. She described being huddled in a corner and terrified that someone was going to kill her. She also began to mention voices in her head. Jessa stayed in the group home for several weeks, then went to a foster home in Oak Harbor. She seemed to adjust well there, and I received an occasional letter letting me know that she was doing okay. She went to Montana with her foster family and found an eagle feather there. She wrote that she knew it was a sign for her that she would return to my home.

A few months later, I got a letter from Jessa telling me she had left the foster home and was living in the University District with a lawyer named Marilyn. Her father had arranged this placement. She was four months pregnant and wanted to know if she could return to my home and continue her pregnancy. The father of her child was a student at the university and though he was not pleased at the prospect of becoming a father, he wanted to be involved and Jessa was sure that he would eventually marry her.

I agreed to take Jessa back during her pregnancy and she returned to my home. She had grown up a lot and had become quite beautiful. This period was one of relative stability for Jessa and she seemed to be growing up. She asked me if I thought she would handle being a single parent. I told her I honestly didn't think she could, explaining that I had seen her give up every time it got hard when she tried to do something. I pointed out that every time a class got hard, she quit. She still believed that because she was so bright, she shouldn't have to work hard at things. Jessa was not happy to hear me say these things and said she would prove to me that I was wrong. I assured her I was very hopeful that she could prove me wrong, but that she would have another life depending on her and she should look at adoption as a possibility.

Jessa got a job as a cashier on the Monorail and had an uneventful pregnancy. She continued her vegetarian lifestyle and only gained 19 lbs. during her pregnancy. She had a healthy baby boy, whom she named after her grandfather and his stepfather. I think this was one final gesture of reconciliation on her part; she hoped her mother would reach out to her and her new grandchild, but that didn't happen.

Jessa did not return to my house after the baby was born. She turned 18 a few days after giving birth and she had arranged to rent a room with some friends close to where her father lived.

The next call from Jessa was about six months later. She told me she had moved in with Adam, the baby's father, had registered for college and was taking her pre-requisites for nursing school. About six months later she called crying. She said Adam had been physically abusing her and that she had dropped out of school because she couldn't handle the pressure. It was almost two years before she called again. She was in San Francisco dancing in a strip club. She had given her son up for adoption. It was an open adoption; she could see her son four times a year and get regular updates on his progress. I knew that Jessa was using drugs again and she said the voices were back in her head, but she was trying not to listen to them. She said the only time she felt safe was in my house.

The next call was a year later. She was in Seattle living in a motel with some guy who was a drug user, and it was clear that Jessa had lost control of every aspect of her life. She came to see me one day and slept on my couch for the weekend. We talked about her going into treatment, but she had lots of reasons why she wasn't ready. The next call came from King County jail. Jessa had been picked up for assault and when she tried to talk to me it was clear that she had suffered a psychotic break. She was shouting at the voices in her head and was completely paranoid. She was sure the phone was tapped, that the government was spying on her, and they were coming to hurt my family and me. She was moved to a psychiatric facility in West Seattle. The calls came every 30 minutes all day, every day, sometimes completely incoherent, sometimes able to talk rationally for a few minutes before the voices would overwhelm her. She was put on medication and detoxed from the street drugs. After two weeks, she went to court and the judge released her. She was out less than 24 hours before being re-arrested and sent back to the facility. She had gone straight back to the drugs. I told her not to call me again until she was clean and sober because I couldn't really help her if she continued to do drugs.

About three months later, I got another call. Jessa was in Chicago living with a young man she had met in drug treatment. She calls now about once a month and she is stable. I'll always pray for Jessa and feel a great sadness for the loss of potential in this lovely young woman. Every night I still say, "God bless Jessa."

Lyla checked in around Christmas. She told me that she had become a Muslim and that I had changed her life. She said she felt more peaceful than she has ever been. She plans to marry a man that she met at Mosque. She loves the structure and finds that covering her hair and arms helps her to focus on what is inside rather than the outside. She also said that she had learned to set clear boundaries and she never allowed anyone in her home who was drinking or smoking. Lyla sounded wonderful.

Betti met a young man from Pennsylvania and went back east with him. Three years ago, they returned to Seattle for about six months. They have a beautiful little girl who is now five years old, and Betti is a day care teacher.

The family situation between Betti and her mother became completely unworkable. As her mother's health deteriorated, she became more abusive and demanding. Finally, Betti said, "Enough," and moved back east to Tennessee. She realized that there was really no hope of salvaging the relationship with her mother and that her first duty was to her husband and daughter. Betti has remained the social director among the four girls. She talks to all the others at least once a month and calls me two or three times a week. These girls are 27 years old now. They are good mothers and productive members of society. It's a good feeling for me to see this, and I hope that Jessa will find her way back, too.

One of the things all these girls had in common was early sexual abuse and failure of the mother to protect them. The result was that they were sexualized at an early age and they thought that their value as women was only for sex. They all felt unloved and would do anything to feel loved and valued even for those few moments when they were being used sexually.

It's so easy to cast stones at young girls who behave this way, to see them as cheap and easy, but this only reinforces their feelings of worthlessness. At least three out of four girls in the foster care system have been sexually abused. They will carry the scars of that abuse their whole lives. Working with these girls requires a great deal of sensitivity and compassion. There are also strict guidelines that I try to follow. Be very careful about touch. Do not hug, pat, or kiss them. The most loving thing you can do is to listen and to talk to them about everything and to give them clear guidelines about what behavior is acceptable and what is not. I talk to the girls about respecting their bodies and getting good medical care, about sexually transmitted diseases and symptoms to pay attention to. One of the first questions I ask is, "Are you on birth control?" If they say no (and most do), I say, "If you are sexually active, I will help you get birth control."

I know a lot of people think that we should just tell kids to practice abstinence. I believe we must deal with the reality of their lives. I talk about bonding with a man we are having sex with and how we sometimes form bonds with inappropriate people and put up with behaviors we would not accept from anyone else because we think we love that person. The reality is we are in bondage with that person. We are glued to, stuck with, enslaved by the bond. The way to avoid this is to avoid sex outside of marriage. It is practical protection so that we have time to really get to know the person before we form that bond.

I challenge the girls to six months of abstinence. "It's a matter of learning to control your own body, deciding to be responsible for your own body and who and when you share it with someone." This is a totally new concept for many of these young women, especially if they are victims of sexual abuse. In Betti's case it was the beginning of her healing, and it changed how she saw herself.

One of the things I tried to do in the receiving home was to make things very predictable. I printed lists for each chore so the girls knew what my expectation was. They knew what time they would get up, when dinner was served and what my expectation was about meals. I never asked a child to eat something they hated, but if they chose not to eat dinner because they didn't like what was served, the other choice was a peanut butter and jelly sandwich and fruit. I did not short-order cook. They had to eat at the table, no food in the rooms. No raiding the kitchen at night. This was the hardest one to enforce. I often dealt with kids who had never had set meal times and they often would steal food and hide it in their room. It was a constant battle to keep on top of this issue.

When we lived in the Finn Hill house, I had a child from Texas placed with me and when I opened her suitcases, the smell was overpowering and several roaches ran from her clothing. This was the beginning of a yearlong battle to rid my house of roaches. It cost several hundred dollars to have the house sprayed over a period of several months, and I had to be ever vigilant that kids did not sneak food downstairs.

Kids in foster care come from all kinds of backgrounds. They may have scabies or lice or there may be bugs in their clothes. A foster parent learns to expect anything and to deal with it in a way that does not shame the child. One of the ways I did that was to say, "While you are here, you must …" and I would try to address whatever the issue was. Some kids had poor hygiene. "While you are here you must shower and wash your hair every day." "While you are here you must hang up your wet towels." "While you are here you must do your laundry twice a week." "While you are here you must clean the tub after you use it!" The list could be very long, but I won't bore you with that. I will say that I used these words, because they did not cast judgment on whatever habits or behaviors that the child used in his family of origin. They were neutral statements of what I expected.

While we were in the Finn Hill house, I took two kids who were sisters. They were Sioux Indians and they were supposed to be with me for 10 days. They were 12 and 14 years old. I didn't take 12-year-olds generally because they are too vulnerable to the behaviors of the kinds of kids I often worked with, but I thought I would give it a try because it was only 10 days. Alene and Lauren arrived and they were polite sweet girls. Lauren, the 12-year-old, was turning 13 in two weeks and she had waist-length black hair and an oval face with large brown eyes that had a slight upward slant to the outside corners. Alene had shorter wavy hair, a hooked nose and freckles. She was not traditionally beautiful, but had an exotic, interesting face that drew attention. She was very protective of her little sister. At the end of 10 days the caseworker informed me that the aunt, who was supposed to take the girls, was unable to do so and another relative was being sought. This process went on for several weeks, as one relative after another did not meet the test of a proper placement.

As each placement fell through, Alene grew more and more resentful. She was very angry that her father would not take them. He was an alcoholic in recovery and had severe heart problems. He also had a wife who refused to allow the girls to live with them. Lauren seemed not to care one way or the other, and she settled in at our house. She liked the structure and predictability. Lauren had fetal alcohol effect and was learning disabled. She had to work very hard at schoolwork because she could not comprehend what she read. She would spend three or four hours every night on homework.

Alene did not have the learning problems, but she had anger management issues. After about six months and two different caseworkers, we decided to keep the girls. In all that time, four years, Alene never bonded with my family in anyway. I became friendly with her older sister and her father, and did what I could to establish some real connection with the family, but this child was not open to any emotional connection. After about three years, she ran away. She asked Lauren to go with her, but Lauren refused. She told Alene that she liked it here because we took good care of her and didn't yell at her. Alene was gone for about seven months. She was on the streets and living with whoever would take her in. She lost a lot of weight and became very depressed. She called one day to talk to Lauren and I asked her when she was coming home. She started crying and said, "I didn't think you would let me come back." I told her I wanted her to be safe and that Lauren really needed her, and she should contact her social worker to get re-placed. She did that and returned to my home that night. We talked about how she was feeling and why she ran. She said she was sick and tired of being in foster care and having to go to court, and people that didn't even know her having control over her life. I told her I understood that and, though I could not change it, I respected her feelings. Alene entered a GED program and earned her GED. I went to her graduation at the Langston Hughes Center. Her father and older sister were there, also, and her mother showed up to see her walk across the stage and get her certificate. I felt so proud of her. It was really special.

During the time these girls were with us, we had to move again. The man who owned the beautiful Finn Hill house became ill and decided to sell his properties. He asked if I wanted to buy the house, but it was way beyond my price range. I was now being paid $25.07 per day for each of my six beds and I was getting a retainer of about $1200 a month, but I could not qualify for a loan on such an expensive house, so we began looking for another place to rent. Finding a rental property big enough, and one I could afford, was problematic, but the biggest issue was that people don't want to rent out their property to be used for a group home for teenagers. They fear that there will be too much damage. There is some justification for those fears.

Once again the fates smiled on me. I found a house in the Kingsgate neighborhood about two miles away from where we were. It was not as large or as nice, but it was in a good neighborhood and in the same school district. It was being remodeled and painted inside and had new carpets throughout. It was a split-level with three bedrooms, two baths, living room, dining room and kitchen upstairs. The lower level had two bedrooms, bath, and a den which could be converted into a dorm bedroom, a laundry room and two-car garage. It had a large flat fenced backyard with an apple tree in the center. When I met with the property manager and told her I wanted to use it for a receiving home, she said, "One of my friends does that!" We signed the lease, got the keys and were told the property would be ready in one week. I gave notice, called the moving company, called DSHS to inform them of the move and started packing.

Moving day dawned cold and raining. I looked outside to find my cul-de-sac filled with heavy equipment. They were digging up the street and we were blocked in. A water main had broken under the street and huge amounts of water were rushing down the hill. They shut off the water, and soon they cut off the electricity too. I called the moving company, canceled the truck and got out the cold cereal and plastic bowls and spoons. It was a very long day.

The next day we tried it again and it went a little better. We got everything moved into the new house, the beds made up and a few things put away. We ordered pizza, ate and fell into bed. I think everyone was asleep five minutes after we went to bed. The next day, I took the kids to school and returned to the house to continue unpacking and getting our new home in order. As the day rushed by and the house was began to look like home.

Shortly after dinner, when we sat down in the living room to take a much-needed break, the house seemed to rise up in the air and fall back with a great thump. Everything started shaking. After a few very long seconds, I realized we were having an earthquake. The girls came screaming upstairs and I told everyone to stand against the wall in the hallway. It was over quickly, but we were all "shook up." I realized I didn't know where the shut off valve to the gas line was, so I told everyone to go outside and wait in the driveway. Lisa and I made a tour of the house and looked for damages. We had a few broken dishes and a crack in the chimney, but otherwise everything seemed to be okay. It was a very long night.

We had been in the house about a month when the spring rains began. The rain was heavy and pouring over the gutters in a waterfall onto the back deck. I called the property manager to send someone out to clean out the gutters because they were blocked. She sent a young man who unblocked the front ones and walked across the roof to get to the back gutters. His foot went through the roof in three places. He told me what had happened and that the roof would have to be replaced. It's not unusual for rain to fall every day in March and April in the Northwest and that's exactly what happened that year. Blue plastic covered the holes in the roof, but the wind blew, and the rain seeped into the roof and dripped through the ceiling into the living room and my bedroom. What a mess! The bedrooms downstairs were cold and drafty. We had to put plastic over the windows and hang insulated drapes to try to keep them warm.

Finally, the rain stopped and the roofers replaced the roof. We lived in that house five years and I never felt like it was a real home. I had decided to go to a maximum of five kids in that house; the place was smaller and just not arranged to allow the privacy for each kid that we had in the Finn

Hill house. We were still in the Juanita High School District, but the Jr. High School was different. I was sorry to leave the Finn Hill Jr. High School because they had been very supportive of me and willing to work with my kids even though they had a lot of problems.

Lauren was the first kid who was placed into Kamiakin Jr. High. She had been there about two weeks when I got a call from the vice-principal that I needed to come in for a conference. Lauren and two other girls had entered the boy's locker room during a baseball game and stolen several belts and some money. Lauren was so unsophisticated that she wore the belt she had stolen to school the next day. When confronted, she admitted taking it. Like a lot of kids with fetal alcohol effect, she didn't have much impulse control and just didn't always connect the dots. Lauren complained that she couldn't see the blackboard, so I took her in for an eye exam. She was so nearsighted that she was unable to see anything clearly that was more than five feet away. We got glasses for her, and she asked for contact lenses for her birthday. With the contacts, her schoolwork improved a lot. She finished eighth grade, received an award for most improved student, and was selected as student of the week two times while she was at Kamiakin.

One of the things that foster kids don't have is a good photographic record of their growing up. I tried to make sure that the kids had pictures. Even school pictures get to be expensive when you are purchasing for five or six kids. For Lauren's birthday, I took her to a photography studio and had several portraits done of her. They were beautiful and we put together an album of the pictures. Shortly after we had them made, her social worker came to the house and Lauren proudly showed her the album. The social worker asked if she could take the album with her and show the pictures to a photographer friend because she felt Lauren might be able to get some work as a model. I was reluctant, but Lauren was excited about the idea and I agreed.

The social worker never brought the album back. After several weeks and several calls, and several promises to return them, the social worker told Lauren she had left them with the photographer and that Lauren should go pick them up. Lauren couldn't find the photographer and she never got her pictures back. That was $250 gone and the dreams of a young girl taken away, and I still don't understand how that social worker could have been that insensitive and careless. She took a part of that child's history and threw it away and completely disregarded that child's feelings.

Lauren had started to date by now and she got involved with a Hispanic boy who was three years older. He was friendly and personable, but I felt he was too old to be dating Lauren. She would say she was going out with her friends and sneak out to see him. She began climbing out the window at night. I was completely unable to change her mind about this boy. I asked her if they were having sex and she admitted they were. I took her to a doctor for birth control and tried to keep her involved in school and positive activities while this romance ran its course. I knew that this boy drank alcohol and that Lauren was starting to use alcohol too. She had introduced this boy to her father and her adult sister; they liked him, and she often met him there even though she knew I did not approve. One night she called me crying and said this boy had left her in downtown Seattle because she was insisting that he bring her home so she wouldn't be late for curfew. He had slapped her and pushed her out of the car.

After that incident, she quit seeing him for a few months and she dated several other boys. She developed a friendship with a boy in the neighborhood and began dating a boy who lived in the house with her friend. I was still concerned about Lauren though, because I knew she was using alcohol fairly regularly. Lauren got a job at the Boys and Girl's Club as a summer camp counselor and she did really well at it. She was working with seven- to nine-year-olds, and every night she would put together her art projects and her written plan for the activities for the following day. That summer was great. It seemed that she had made a decision to get back on track. We were very proud of her efforts and let her know how well she was doing.

Shortly after Lauren entered the tenth grade at Juanita High School, she resumed using alcohol and began hanging out with "Edwardo," who was the brother of her old boyfriend. I got a call one morning about 11:00 AM from the Kirkland Police Department asking me to come pick Lauren up. They had her and several other teens in custody for "minor in possession" charges. The police had been called to a residence in Kirkland because someone, "Edwardo," was in the backyard shooting a gun. He had been target practicing in a residential area, and when they investigated, they found several teens in the house drunk. Lauren was suspended from school for a week and was grounded for a week and given work hours to complete.

About three weeks later, there was a drive-by shooting across out street and down a couple of houses. It was at the home of Lauren's friend, Tony. No one was hurt, but two bullets penetrated the house and of course we were all concerned. These kinds of things don't usually happen in this neighborhood.

Lauren seemed too quiet and depressed and was staying home a lot during this time. One night about 11 o'clock, she came into my room and asked if she could talk to me. She told me that on the night of the shooting, she had crawled out the bathroom window and met Edwardo and two other guys. They were all drinking and decided to drive by the house of Tony and Carlos and shoot out Carlos' tires because of some issue they had with him. When they got to the house, the young men started arguing about who was going to do the shooting. Lauren said she was really scared and just wanted to leave, but they kept arguing. She picked up the gun and held it out the window, pointing up in the air, and fired the gun twice. The young men gunned the engine and got out of the area. They yelled at her for being really stupid and brought her home. I held her in my arms and she cried and cried. I told her I had to call the police and report what she had told me, but I'd do whatever I could to help her. The police came and interviewed her, put her in handcuffs and took her to the station, where she was booked, fingerprinted and taken to Juvenile Detention.

The prosecuting attorney decided to charge her as an adult because there was a weapon involved and, because she had confessed, they had an open and shut case. The young men involved vanished into places unknown, and no one but Lauren was ever arrested. She was charged with reckless endangerment and was looking at the possibility of three years in prison.

I did everything I could to help her. I went to her old school and got letters from the vice-principal and teachers and school counselors. I got letters from the people who worked with her at the Boys and Girls Club. I wrote a letter to the judge on her behalf. All of this helped and she was given 30 days detention and two years probation. She did, however, now have a criminal record of a violent crime, and this will haunt her forever. Lauren was not allowed to return to my home at that time, but was placed in Aloha House, a group home in Seattle. After that she was released to her older sister because she was almost 18. She stayed in touch and seemed to be doing well. She enrolled in the GED program at Shoreline Community College and completed her high school education. She began working as a hostess in a restaurant, but she was unable to handle waitressing because she couldn't memorize the menus. After several job changes, two or three failed relationships, and the loss of her father from a heart attack, she went to Hawaii to live with Alene and Alene's boyfriend, Jack, and their three-year-old daughter.

A few months later Lauren and Alene came to Seattle for Christmas. Lauren told me she was five months pregnant and she was staying with a friend, but could only stay there through the end of the month and would then be homeless. She was working at World Wraps, but not making enough to get a place of her own. She had decided to continue her pregnancy. I talked with my son, Jason, about Lauren's situation and he agreed to let her stay with him for a few weeks. He had an extra bedroom and we moved her in there. His girlfriend wasn't thrilled with that, but after meeting Lauren, she realized that Jason regarded Lauren as a little sister and that we needed to help her. She moved in and that worked well and bought a little time to try to find a suitable situation for Lauren. She enrolled in college again and continued working, and I contacted "Friends of Youth" about their program for young single mothers. She was accepted and moved into their program about three weeks before her baby was due. She had a lovely two-bedroom apartment that was subsidized and she only had to pay 30% of her income for rent and utilities. I got a call from her in early May saying she was in labor and asking me to come to the hospital. I went to be with her and I was there when her daughter was born. I cut the cord and said a prayer for this new life. Lauren was afraid to return to her apartment alone with the new baby, so I brought her home with me for two weeks. I didn't ask anyone's permission. I knew that it would not be approved, but I also knew she needed help and had no one to help her. So I did it. The baby was beautiful and sweet natured like her mother and after a couple of weeks, Lauren seemed okay, so we took her home to her apartment. She did well with the baby and made friends with other young mothers in the complex. Things went well for several months and Lauren and the baby visited often. Lauren went to work part-time in a fast food restaurant, but she had problems with day care. She often had to work weekends and evenings and no day care was available, so she started letting her mother baby-sit for her. This was problematic because her mother suffered from bipolar disorder and, though she was currently stable, Lauren was afraid that it wasn't a safe situation. She remembered her own childhood, and how her mom had been with her and her sister. One of the girls in the apartment complex lost her baby to SIDS; that seemed to be a huge loss for Lauren also. She started showing signs of severe depression and seemed to lose interest in everything. I think she was prescribed antidepressants, but did not respond to them. She became actively suicidal and was hospitalized and diagnosed with bipolar disorder. I think Lauren had begun to drink alcohol again and this may have contributed to her downward slide.

Lauren came to see me to let me know she had gotten "Section 8" housing in Everett and was moving the following weekend. She said she would call and give me her new phone number in a week, but she didn't call. It's been two years and I've not heard from her. I pray for her and ask God to keep her and Raylene safe. It's hard not knowing.

Dear Rita,

Thank you for helping me when I needed it. You were there, telling me I was ok when I wasn't sure I had a reason to keep trying. You never involved yourself in my life and the problems I was having at home. You make me feel like I was smart and pretty and special. I needed that a lot. I know now that I'm going to be handling my life.

Thank you, Shawna

DURING THESE YEARS, A LOT OF CHANGES were happening with the Department of Children's Services. Administrators came and went, and each one tried to make the huge unwieldy system function a little better or more efficiently. Budget cuts and lack of money to provide needed services are always a problem.

I got a call from my placement desk one day, and Beth mentioned in casual conversation that the CRC beds had been eliminated and the retainers cancelled. I hit the ceiling! "What! You mean that my retainer and my program have been eliminated and no one even bothered to inform me! No letter, no phone call, nothing! So, I am just supposed to find out when my check comes that I now have $900 a month less money to operate this home? Gee, thanks for the consideration!!!" Poor Beth was caught in the middle. She did not know I had not been notified.

The next week one of the area managers called and told me why the program had been cut and that there were only three homes affected. She was sorry I had not been notified, but the family CRC program had been eliminated. She did tell me that my retainer would be raised on my other beds, so I would actually only lose about $400 a month. Thanks a lot!

There was also talk within the system that the After Hours Placement Office would be closed. This was difficult to hear because we (all foster parents) knew that we could always call the After Hours Unit if we had a problem. If a child was out of control or two kids were fighting and one needed to be removed, we could, and did, call After Hours. They would come pick up the kid and find a new placement for them. If the police removed a child from a home during the night or weekend, that child was taken to After Hours where a social worker would interview them and find a temporary home for them. At least half of my placements came from the After Hours Unit. That's why I am paid a retainer. I am "on call" to receive children 24 hours a day, seven days a week.

The new plan was to have a call center that would cover the whole state and the police would take the kids directly to the homes. When this plan was developed, no one bothered to check with the local police departments to see if they were willing to do this. They weren't! There were meetings and focus groups and delays in implementing the plan. One of the issues was that some law officers have huge rural areas to cover, and the lack of manpower made it impossible for them to transport kids. They would possibly have children en route when they were called to deal with violent situations. They refused to even consider it.

The next idea was to have a social worker on call that would pick up kids and transport them to foster homes. This didn't work very well because the statewide call center was not familiar with local resources. After a year of this it became clear that the statewide call center was unworkable and the various regions went back to local call centers with local caseworkers doing the actual physical placements. The net result is that if a foster parent has a problem, they may have to wait several hours to have a child removed from their home.

Changes always create other changes. The loss of After Hours as a functioning unit caused me to refuse a lot of kids who has a history of assault or property damage. Another change is children have no place to go to "self refer" outside of the "40-hour work week."

When there was an actual building with people in it, a child in trouble, "a runaway" who wanted to turn themselves in, or a child put out by parents could, and did, go there for help. If a child was picked up by police, they were taken to that building to wait to be interviewed and, hopefully, placed in a receiving home.

The new system is less expensive and many less children are placed. One has to ask, "Is this because there is less need, or is it just less resources?"

In this narrative, I have mentioned several caseworkers in a critical way and I want to make sure that I do not leave the impression that most people in social services are thoughtless or uncaring. The very opposite is true. Most people are drawn to this kind of work because they truly want to help children and take their work very seriously. Some people have a natural grace under pressure that makes them really outstanding. They seem to be able to manage the long hours, huge case loads, court appointments that take all day to get 10 minutes before a judge, the endless driving, uncooperative clients, and negative media attention and still work for the best interest of the child. What makes them stand out in my mind? They all have a true understanding of the reality of the kids' lives. They are kind and caring, but not to the point of being manipulated or used. They are professionals of the highest order. They are team players who go by the rules and expect the same from everyone who works with the kids on their case load. They are role models and authority figures for the kids, and they do wondrous things with little recognition and not much compensation. They also respect what foster parents do and make us feel like a part of the team.

There was great concern among people who worked with foster kids about how ill prepared they were to face responsibility. Most kids who grow up with their biological parents can count on some help as they make that transition. Foster kids are expected to make it with no help. They are woefully unprepared to do so.

My daughter, Lisa, and I developed a program where we taught skills like financial management and banking, as well as job search and community resource knowledge. We also required the girls to spend five hours a week learning computer skills. The kids were required to find a part-time job and to save at least $50 a month. I matched what they saved and it was put into a savings account that required both the teen's signature as well as my own to withdraw from the account. The girls were also given $50 a month that they must spend on household items. These were collected and stored so they would have a head start on getting an apartment set up. The state funded this program for two of my five beds, and the stipulation was that the kids had to be long-term and sign a participation contract.

This program worked very well and I helped several kids emancipate. I thought I had finally developed something very solid and workable, but I was not the only person who knew foster kids need these things. There was a bill in Congress called the Chaffee Bill, which addressed the needs of foster kids as they aged out of the system. This bill provided money to the states to set up transitional programs and teach basic survival skills. When the money became available, the larger youth service agencies quickly put together programs and my program was cut. I still felt very good about my program. One of my kids had $1800 in her account and all her kitchen, bath and bedroom supplies when she turned 18.

The biggest issue facing most kids when they age out of the system is medical care. In the Seattle area, there are several low cost or free clinics that provide basic health services, but if a young person has a real health crisis they are in trouble. Many of these young people have mental health issues, and there are few services for them and no help to pay for expensive medications. When these young people turn 18, they often have to come off the medications that have kept them stable because they can't afford them, and they become non-functional as their conditions deteriorate. They lose their ability to work and they end up homeless.

When we lived in the house on 129th Place, there were several kids who came to live with us who are etched in my memory and my heart.

LeeAnn was 15 when she was placed with me the first time. She had light red-blond hair, big green eyes and very white skin. She was extremely thin, had low energy and spoke in a voice so soft that I could not understand her. She was one of eight children being raised in a two-bedroom trailer. Her father had not worked in years. He was controlling and regularly abused the mother who was the sole support of the family. I believe there was sexual abuse of the girls, though there were no charges ever filed.

LeeAnn was bright and did well in school, but I often had to go pick her up because she was feeling faint. It became clear to me that LeeAnn had a serious eating disorder. I got her into counseling and set up a program for her: she had to take three bites of breakfast and drink a small glass of juice or milk. She had to sit at the table during dinner, eat six bites of food and drink a glass of milk or juice. This went on for several months and she began to gain a little weight.

She was in an abusive relationship with a young man who had helped her to leave home. She felt a lot of loyalty to him because he had been there for her in the struggle to get away from her father. She did not see that she had traded one abuser for another. One of the good things in LeeAnn's life was her relationship with her mother. Her mother had gone back to college and was pursuing a nursing degree. This gave LeeAnn hope that there was a way out. She often met with her mother on weekends or evenings and they had a chance to strengthen their relationship outside of the control of the father. LeeAnn began to relax and she became playful and supportive with the other kids in the home. She formed a strong bond with my grandson, Josh, and would spend hours building Lego houses and playing with his superhero figures on the living room floor. I think this was a healing time for her and she was able to "get back" some of her earlier childhood in a safe environment.

After several months, it was decided that LeeAnn would go to Utah where she would live with her aunt and her family. They had several children and lived in a small town. They were very involved in the Mormon Church and were good citizens in their community. LeeAnn stayed in Utah about nine months and was asked to leave her aunt's home because she would not go by the family rules. She had come home several times with alcohol on her breath and had been caught with marijuana in her purse.

When the social worker called and asked if I would take her back, I agreed to do so. She returned to my home a few months before entering the twelfth grade. She was determined to graduate on time and she did! She managed to maintain her grades even with a part-time job during her senior year. She was still very thin, but was eating and her health improved. The abusive boyfriend had joined the Marines and was no longer in the area. She met a young man who was attending one of the prep schools in Seattle. The son of a foreign diplomat, he began a serious courtship of LeeAnn. He took her out to expensive restaurants, brought her roses, taught her to play tennis and bought her expensive tennis shoes and a high quality racket. The more he pursued, the more uncomfortable she became and eventually she broke off the relationship.

She told me that never had anyone treat her so well, and she knew she really didn't deserve that kind of treatment. She said that when his family took a look at her family, they would run screaming in the other direction. She didn't want to deal with all that, so it was better to stop it now. It made her uncomfortable, she said, to have someone care about her.

LeeAnn graduated from high school and aged out of the system. She had become involved in the YMCA independent living program and they helped her to find housing. It was hard keeping a job, and over the next two years, she had several low-paying positions. She met a young man and began a serious relationship. She got pregnant and they married. Her mother graduated from nursing school and got a job and a divorce.

LeeAnn stayed in contact. She had a beautiful little boy that she brought over to see us on a regular basis. She also got into counseling and began the serious work of getting over her abusive past. LeeAnn's husband was called back into military service and they are now living in Texas. She called recently to tell me she is expecting her second child and that her son would start kindergarten in the fall. She thanked me for being there and told me that she was a better parent because she had lived in my home, and would always remember how I had given her a sense of being someone who had some value. When I get a call like that, I know that I have made a difference, and that it's all worth it.

Jeanette came in the middle of the night, and I think I scared her half to death before she even walked through the front door. I had received the call about her about 9:00 PM, but the cab got her to my house about 1:30 AM. When I opened the door, the cab driver began to berate me for giving bad directions. He complained they had been driving around for an hour-and-a-half all over Juanita and Finn Hill trying to find my house. I countered that the problem was he couldn't, or didn't, follow my directions, which were to turn neither left nor right when he came off the freeway, but to proceed through the light; if he had done that, he would not have ended up on Finn Hill. He muttered and sputtered and wanted to argue more, but I saw the fright in the child's face and realized she didn't need to hear two adults arguing. So I told him it was a common mistake and I was glad he finally found me, then asked for the papers and took the child upstairs. My first impression of Jeanette was that she could make a living as a double for Marilyn Monroe, but she was more fit and her hair was a beautiful natural light blond and almost to her waist. I looked at her intake form and it listed her age as 13. She looked 21. It wasn't that she looked hardened or was wearing too much makeup or dressed inappropriately, but that she had a D-cup bust, tiny waist, full hips and long legs. The intake form said she had run away from her step-grandfather. She had been removed from her mother's custody along with her siblings because of severe abuse and neglect. She had lived in a foster home for about four years. At that time her father got himself clean and sober and took custody of the kids. He and his girlfriend and all the kids moved into the home of the girlfriend's parents, where they did well for a few years. Then, Jeanette's father was killed in a trucking accident. Left in the custody of the step-grandparents, the kids ran wild. There were several CPS reports filed, but no action taken. The step-grandmother had died three months ago and there were allegations that the grandfather was making sexual grooming moves to Jeanette. She ran away and stayed with a friend for two weeks, but now she had no place to go. I made her welcome, got her a T-shirt to sleep in, some towels, soap and toothbrush and took her downstairs to bed. The next morning she woke up and got acquainted with the other girls. She told them stories about how she liked to fight and how tough she was and how she had worked in an Italian restaurant as a waitress. I overheard some of the stories and told her I knew she was just a scared little kid and it was okay. I made plans to take her to school to register for class. She confessed to me that she had not gone to school for six months, that she had failed seventh grade, and she wasn't going back into seventh grade. I agreed that she could not fit into a seventh grade environment, and I'd see what I could do. I went to school and talked with the school counselor, and it was agreed to put her into ninth grade with special education services. She was surprised and very happy that I had been able to make that happen. She did well at Kamiakin. She had a serious attitude problem and continued to play the tough girl. She managed to take the leadership position with the other girls in the home, partly because they were a little afraid of her. She obeyed the rules in the house and was quite helpful to me and we developed a funny kind of relationship. She said one day that I was too old to be called Rita. I asked her what she wanted to call me. She thought about it and said "I'll just call you Old Woman." I said, "Okay, I'll just call you Punk Kid." She laughed and said that was okay, so for the next few months she would come bouncing through the door and say, "Hi, Old Woman!" I'd answer, "Hi, Punk Kid, how was your day?" She would tell me stories about what she had done in school that day. She also had big stories to tell about how she had traveled to many places and about her father and how he had taken care of her.

Jeanette had a social worker who clearly did not get along with her. Jeanette was disrespectful and threatening and often verbally abusive. The more abusive she became the more the social worker tried to gain control. The more controlling the social worker became, the more abusive Jeanette became. She threatened to blow up the DSHS office. The social worker refused to return her calls, and one day Jeanette asked me for her social worker's supervisor's name and number. I gave it to her and asked why she needed it. She replied she wanted to try to get a change to another worker. About three days later, I got a call from the social worker at 7:00 AM. She was yelling that I had no right to give that kid her supervisor's name and number, and she had been reprimanded by her supervisor and she felt I was completely out of line. I told her that it was not only my responsibility, it was written in the WAC code that this information be given any client that asks for it. It was also written that the social worker should visit the home and speak with the child every two months, and that social worker never once visited my home.

Jeanette stayed about six months, then ran away with another kid who had serious drug problems. She was gone about nine months. One day, she turned herself in for placement again and they called to see if I would take her back. I agreed and she came back. She was thin and worn looking, and she told me she had been living with some drug dealers and had become addicted to cocaine. She said the guy had become physically abusive, that he threatened to kill her and had cut her arm with a knife. She said that one day she woke up and realized that nothing would change unless she changed it. She quit drugs cold turkey, and went and stayed in Everett for three weeks while she got clean, and said that she didn't want that kind of life. She wanted to be a policewoman. She said, "Thanks for taking me back, Nana." That's what my grandson calls me. She never called me Old Woman again.

We started over. I got her enrolled in an alternative school because I knew she would never fit into the regular high school environment. Jeanette had a problem reading. Her math skills weren't very good either. It was because she had missed so much school, and her life had been so chaotic that she had no emotional energy to learn. The school she was in was for homeless and street kids. The crowd was rough and there were problems almost daily with fights. Jeanette's attitude was hard for the teachers to deal with, but they offered her a lot of support and they had a lot of outside activities that were very enriching. She got to go to horse camp and an outward-bound program. She got to go sailing on a tall ship. Jeanette grew in confidence and her natural strength became more evident. She had a very strong work ethic, and she proved herself to be a valuable employee. She began working at McDonald's. She was soon opening and closing and working too many hours to be legal. I got her involved in the Police Explorers. She loved it and went to every meeting. She was soon directing traffic at festivals and helping out in many ways. She looked so good in that uniform.

Jeanette's anger problems got her in trouble at school a lot. One day, I sat down with her to talk about what was going on in her life. I told her that I knew she had lots of reasons to be angry, that most people would not have survived what she had, and her anger was really her strength. I told her that she could use her anger or let it destroy her. She was a fighter and not afraid to work hard for what she wanted. She admitted to me that when she came to my house she could not read and that she often blew up in school because she didn't want people to know she couldn't read very well. We started working to improve her skills; soon she was reading and her writing skills were quite good. She wrote a lot of poems and short stories and did a lot of journaling. She also started learning to use the computer. She quit working at McDonalds and went to work at Jiffy Lube as a service technician.

The alternative school had a prom for the kids at the local ballroom and we went shopping for a prom dress. We decided on a light blue dress with thin straps and a simple long straight skirt with a side slit. She was so beautiful. She looked like a movie star. She got her GED and got a better job and moved in with her older sister. She has continued to work hard and I know she will survive.

I look at Jeanette and marvel at what she had to overcome, from being chained with a dog chain to deprivation of the worst kind. The foster family who took the kids originally reported that they were completely wild. They would steal food and hide it in their beds and they would yell, spit, punch and scratch anyone who tried to discipline them. She survived the loss of her father, her step-grandmother, lack of schooling, lack of support. She kicked a drug habit and walked out on an abusive relationship. All this before she was 18. She proves the resiliency of the human spirit better than any other kid I ever worked with. I love this young woman like my own child and I'm glad I was there when she needed a helping hand. She moved to Florida and then to California. She stays in touch and I am immensely proud of the woman she has become.

The Department of Children's Services hired a consulting firm and paid them a huge amount of money to design a system to standardize the payment system for foster care. The system that existed was a negotiation of each case between the foster parent and the social worker and it was based on the child's past history of difficulty in managing the behaviors. There were problems with this because payments varied so greatly from home to home.

I was often asked to take kids into my home for receiving care when they blew out of long-term care. Sometimes the last foster parent had been paid $3,000 a month for that child's care. Unbelievably, I was paid $25 a day to care for the same child. These children often stayed three to five months in my home. Some of the behaviors foster parents were expected to deal with were extreme. A child might have a history of extreme aggression or property damage and mental health issues, or gang involvement with a heavy criminal history. Some of the kids needed a support worker who helped the foster parent manage the behaviors. Some of the kids were just oppositional-defiant-disordered and required a lot of skill on the part of the foster parent.

The problem with trying to design a standard system of payment is that the kids don't fit into neat little boxes. The plan that the consultants devised listed six categories:

1. Physical needs.

2. Behavioral needs.

3. Educational needs.

4. Arranging, scheduling and supervising activities.

5. Chronic conditions, destructive behaviors.

6. Preparing for transition.

We are supposed to estimate the time we spend on each activity and the payment level is gauged from 1 to 4, depending on the scale and time spent. Level 1 is basic foster care with none of the problems and that is $575 per month. Out of that payment, we are expected to give the child $50 a month for clothing and $50 a month for allowance. That leaves $414 to provide food and all housing costs, like water, heat, laundry, school fees, transportation, recreation and the hundreds of other needs children have. For teen girls, those things include makeup, hair products, personal hygiene products, and school supplies.

The State of Washington has custody of many of these children. The state's level of support is so low that it's well below the poverty line. It's no mystery why these children grow up with poor self-esteem.

This level system also punishes the most skilled and rewards the least skilled foster parents. I am good at working with oppositional-defiant-disordered kids. I can often de-escalate a conflict in 10 minutes that might take a less experienced foster parent hours to do. Measuring the hours I spend de-escalating does not take into account the time I spend getting to really know the child, so I know what currency to use with that child. It rewards failure and punishes success. Many good, highly skilled foster parents left the system because of the unfairness of this. It also means that every six months you must go through this rate assessment, and if you are succeeding with a child, your payment will be cut. It ignores the fact that when a child feels comfortable enough, they will start to deal with past trauma. They need a supportive environment to do this. It does not address the foster parent's part in creating a healing environment where the child feels safe and valued and respected.

Many foster parents have chosen to make raising other people's children a life work. We do it from our hearts. It is a ministry and we believe we are changing the world, one child at a time. We have no retirement, no social security, no health coverage, no respect from the general population, no understanding of the level of difficulty of the job, and we put our reputation on the line every day because we can be charged with child abuse and neglect, which is a crime. Our homes are damaged by these kids, our cars get stolen, our purses get stolen, our appliances get damaged from improper use or overuse. One day I found my vacuum cleaner in pieces on the floor. One of the kids had sucked up an earring while cleaning her room and got the screwdriver and dismantled the vacuum trying to find her earring. It was not salvageable and had to be replaced. I've had kids load the washing machine so tight the agitator can't work, or pack the dryer with so many clothes that the dryer overheats, or wash two items in a full load setting using too much water. I've had kids take such long showers that they use all the hot water up. These are the kinds of things we deal with, but these are not built into the level system.

One of my friends had a child take red spray paint and spray her walls and carpets. I've had kids take hot pans off the stove and place them on the counter, leaving a burn mark in the countertop. I've had kids begin to cook something, then the phone rings and they forget the pan on the stove, only remembering when the smoke alarm goes off.

There is now a big push in the state to eliminate receiving care and this is creating problems. The prior plan allowed a child to remain in the temporary receiving care for 90 days with a one-month extension if it were in the best interest of the child. This allowed time for a social worker to really "work the case" and it also allowed time to assess the behaviors of the child. We could enroll the child in school and help them with transitions. In February of this year, someone in the Department of Children's Services cut the time a child could be in receiving care to 15 days. At the end of 15 days, we are supposed to roll the kid over to long-term care at basic rates of $514 a month. They also cut our retainers to $112 a month. When the 15 days are up, we lose our retainer and go to basic foster care rate, no matter what the child's behavior is, while a rate assessment is done. This means the caseworker has no incentive and no time to form a case plan that is in the best interest of the child. It also reduces the payment that we receive by about $400 a month per bed. I know the state has a large shortfall in children's services, but this seems unwise. It will burn out more resources and will also force the moves of more children. Each move is a disruption and it has been proven that this causes psychological damage to the child.

In the Braun decision, the state settled a lawsuit addressing some of the issues of foster children being moved unnecessarily and the damage this causes. They agreed to pay damages and to set up services to cut down on moving children unnecessarily. They agreed on oversight to monitor how they are doing and to make funds available to reduce caseloads. From my perspective, what is happening now is in direct violation of that court order. I have a 17-year-old pregnant girl in my home that was moved from her last placement because of payment reductions. According to current guidelines, she can stay here two weeks and will need to be moved again. Two weeks is not long enough to get her into any of the programs that might work for her as a teen parent.

There was an article in the Post Intelligencer about the reduction in foster care rates for people who work with sexually aggressive youth. It described some of the behaviors that these foster parents have to deal with. Some of these kids require "line of sight" supervision and they require alarms on their bedroom windows and doors. Their TV program and read-ing materials must be monitored. They require extensive therapy and must be monitored constantly. One mid-level administrator made the statement that caring for these kids is not a real job and was never meant to take the place of real work. He said people who care for these sexually aggressive youth had become dependent on the money they receive to care for these kids and they need to get real jobs. Some of them are paid $3,000 a month to care for these kids and that's too much, he said.

I was so angry after reading that article in the paper that I wrote a letter to the editor. He did not run it in the paper. The shortsighted attitude of administrators who think what we do is of little value is hard to take. If these children aren't monitored constantly, they may re-offend against a neighborhood child and then the foster parent and the state will be liable. The only way to have these kids in a "least restrictive" setting is to pay someone to be available 24 hours a day. The other alternative is to place these kids in secure facilities with round-the-clock staff coverage. That is a more expensive alternative. In spite of what the administrators think, caring for these children is a very important and very real job. Those of us who take on these responsibilities need to be paid enough to provide a home for these children and to stay at home to do this important work.

There are bad foster parents! They get their names in the paper and we all suffer from the bad publicity. They are few and far between. Most people doing this work really care about children and want to make a difference. These children deserve a home that is nurturing and foster parents that are skilled in helping these children to grow past their trauma and become productive adults. It can be done, and is being done, every day by foster parents all over this country. It's time for the general public to have a clearer understanding of what it is we do. We need the support of the community, the schools and the legislature in order to continue to provide these services.

Raising other people's children can be rewarding because you know you make a difference in the lives of these kids. It is hard work and it should be respected much more than it is. We are paid less than dog groomers because of attitudes like the administrator who says this isn't a real job. These are real kids and their needs are real!

Mom-

Hi, I hope you have a wonderful mother's day and I want you to know how much I love you and how much you mean to me. You are my best friend and my "real" mom. I'm very lucky to have a person like you who puts others above and takes other people into their home and heart. Someone to show them they are worthwhile and there are people who still care about them and you do that for the girls who come into your home and they thank you as well as me. Thank you from the bottom of my heart and God only knows where I would be if you did not take me into your home and give me a second chance. I'm a very lucky person to have had you be my "mom." I love you for that.

Love, Marie

Over a period of 20 years, I have had children from many other countries, Mexico, Columbia, Chile, Haiti, Surinam, Puerto Rico, Norway, India, Somalia, Bosnia, Vietnam, Philippines, and Thailand. These children present special challenges. There is often a language barrier and always a cultural gap, which must be overcome in order to understand the child.

The child from Haiti was 15, three months pregnant and spoke only French. She was also suffering from severe morning sickness. Imagine what this child must have felt. She came from a country so poor that shoes and soap are considered luxury items. She is in a country where no one understands her and she is sick and pregnant. She is placed in a home in an upscale neighborhood. Put yourself in her place: The food is unfamiliar, and the smells are unfamiliar. You can't communicate and you don't know what is expected of you and you don't know why you are here or for how long!

This child was scared to death. She cried and puked and stayed huddled in her covers in bed because she was cold. I made ginger tea for her and she knew what that was. Her face lit up and she smiled and said, "Merci."

I had spoken Cajun French as a child and I remembered a few phrases. Slowly we tried to communicate with words, gestures, sign language, and good will. I became concerned about her becoming dehydrated because she was vomiting so much and eating so little. I took her to the Emergency Room at Evergreen Hospital and one of the doctors there spoke a little French. She was able to communicate with the child enough to explain the procedure of drawing her blood and hooking up the IV fluids. I held her hand and talked to her in English in a soothing voice and hoped the tone of my voice would let her know that we were trying to help her. She was with me for three weeks before World Vision found a suitable home where she was placed. I often wonder about what she thought and felt about that time in my home. I try to imagine what it must have been like for her. I think it was terrible.

I've had several children from Somalia and there is one cultural difference that was hard for me to understand. These children would tell you what they thought you wanted to hear. It had nothing to do with fact or truth as we know it. At first, I didn't understand that in their home culture this was a way of being polite. This is a major cultural difference and takes some getting used to. Many of these children are Muslim and I had to learn about what was acceptable. I found this varied a lot between cultures. The children from Bosnia were not required to cover their arms. They could pray twice a day. They could wear Western-style dress as long as it was modest and they covered their hair and forehead. Some of the African children practiced a mix of dress, some in full Chadri and some more relaxed. Some practiced their religion by prayer five times a day and some did not. Many of the girls were "in care" because, as they tried to fit into Western society, they tried to move away from their upbringing, and they were beaten for it. The parents of these children often don't understand that this is a crime in this country. They are trying to control their children in ways that have always been acceptable in their home country and they are angry and resentful of the state for intervening in what they consider their rightful actions as a parent to raise their children in their own culture.

Some things are universal with all children. They want to be accepted for who they are. They want to be valued. They want to know what you expect from them. They want to know that they can achieve something in their life. I believe all children dream of a better future. It is our job to nurture those dreams and give them the skills to make that future happen.

Maria was a 17-year-old girl who came from Columbia. She had been removed from her home for ongoing domestic violence. She and her family had left Columbia when Maria was nine. They had gone to Surinam and then to the United States. Maria was fluent in Spanish, Dutch, and English., a very good student and with hopes and dreams of becoming a doctor. She had witnessed her father abusing her mother for years. Her mother was passive and unable to see any other choice but to stay in the abusive relationship. Maria had become involved with a young Native American man and the father tried to force Maria to end the relationship. She refused and her father went to the young man and threatened him. The young man broke off the relationship and told Maria they needed to date other people. She became enraged and assaulted the young man. She was arrested and charged with assault. It was at that point the state became involved and she was placed in my home. She continued to pursue a relationship with the boyfriend, Eric, though by this time he had started dating other girls. She would go to his home and try to kick in the door. She was meeting with a counselor, but seemed to have no insight into the situation. On some level, she had decided to model the father's controlling, abusive behavior. She made the statement several times that she would never be a victim like her mother. She followed Eric, threatened the girl he was dating and continued to show up at his home and demand to be let in. The boyfriend's mother went to court and had a restraining order written to try and stop her.

One night about 8:00 PM, the doorbell rang and I answered it. There was a process server at the door and he asked if I was Loreita Richards. I said yes and he handed me a piece of paper. I opened it and was shocked to find that the restraining order had my name on it. Maria's name was not on the order at all. The order restrained me from coming within 500 ft. of the mother of the boy and from contacting the boy in any way by phone, letter or in person. I 'hit the ceiling.' "What! I don't even know these people! I've never seen the mother, I'm not harassing anyone. Why is my name on this order?" I called the court, I wrote to the judge, I called the area manager of DCFS. I was finally told by a court clerk that my name was on it because I was "**In facto** parents," or acting parent of this minor and there was nothing I could do to have my name removed. Her name didn't appear on the document at all and therefore had no legal effect on her. I always thought this was wrong information, but I was unable to prove it or change it, so I wrote a lot of letters, just in case this surfaced at some future date.

Shortly after this incident, Maria was returned home with counseling services provided for the family. This lasted a few weeks and she was removed from the home again. I did not take her back. I got a call a few weeks later from the boyfriend's mother. She said Maria was continuing to harass her and her son, but I told her I had no contact with Maria and didn't know where she was placed. This is another clear example of children learning what they live. Maria had decided not to be a victim, but she became an abuser instead, because those are the two roles she saw and didn't know there was another choice.

One day I received a call from the Department of Licensed Resources. The worker told me that it had come to her attention that I had an 18-year-old living in my home and she would have to have a criminal history check done. I explained to her that the young woman had turned 18 on the 3rd of the month and her placement would end on the 30th. She could remain in placement through the end of the month because she had not graduated. She is scheduled to graduate on the 20th. She told me it didn't matter, she still had to have a criminal history on file. This young woman was a dependent ward of the state. She had been in foster care for years. The system has her records. If she was not a menace to the other children at 17 years, 364 days, why would she become one on her 18th birthday and for the next 27 days she is to remain in my home? There is no exercise of common sense anymore and no one seems able to exercise judgment, so a lot of money gets spent doing these kinds of things. The budget deficit is on everyone's mind, but no one can stop the leaks.

I received a call a few hours later from my placement coordinator regarding my reimbursements for bus tickets. She told me that the fiduciary specialist didn't want to pay it because they had changed the system. Never mind the fact that we have done it that way for 18 years. I understand that procedures need to be updated and changed, but wouldn't you think that the people who are most impacted should be notified of the change. I was not told of the new procedure. My placement coordinator wasn't told. That shows a complete lack of respect for us foster parents. This is just one more example of why I have very mixed feelings about compartmentalizing the various parts of a system like Children's Services. The departments make changes and the information never gets passed down to us. We have no voice in the current administration.

The new system consists of my placement coordinator bringing books of bus tickets to me and I must keep a log sheet and kids must sign it every time they are given a bus ticket. This is one more example of not thinking about the impact of how this will make the kids feel. It's just one more thing that sets them apart.

We did get notice that we would get a raise this year. We will get a 1% raise. This is the first raise in four years and the cost of living keeps going up. For my receiving home beds, that is about 28 cents a day per child.

When a kid grows up in foster care, they are caught in the classic catch 22. They grow up expecting the basic necessities to be provided. They have no sense of responsibility to make the home in which they live prosper in any way. There is no sense of pride in it, there is no feeling of ownership of anything, but there is a sense of entitlement. They don't have work skills, they don't know how the world works and they often don't know how to use basic resources. When they age out of the system, they often have no marketable skills and can't even fill out an application. Many can't read above a grade school level, over half have not completed high school. The ones who make a successful transition to adulthood do so because of grit and determination. We have to do a better job.

Every foster parent who has been raising other people's children has heard the refrain, "You can't tell me what to do. You aren't my real parent. You don't care about me. You're just doing this for the money." "My real mother doesn't make me do that!" "I don't have to stay here. I could just run away!" "I've got friends I could go live with." These are all baiting statements and to respond and try to defend yourself and your motives is useless. I usually respond by saying, "I require a lot from you because I think you are worth it. I believe in who you are and who you can become. I know your life has been hard. You can use your anger or you can let it destroy you. That is your choice. Only you can make it, only you can live it, but my job is to help you get the skills to have a good life. I'm not your mother. I'm here because I want to be and I'll do the best I can. You need to let me know what you need and why you are angry."

Another thing foster parents hear a lot is: "I hate my mother." I respond to that by saying, "Not every parent has the skills to raise children, but one thing you can thank your mother for is she gave you life. You are here because she chose to carry you. I don't know why your mom is not here for you right now. One day she may be able to be, but for now, I'm here to help you grow up. You have a responsibility to do the best you can and be the best you can be. You don't have to live your mother's life. You have to live this one and you can change it by your own hard work. The greatest power you can ever have is to get to where you can say, "I can do it myself." When you can say that, the world will change for you in a positive way. The choices you make then will be your own desires. They will not be made from fear and weakness. You will not accept bad treatment from anyone and you will demand and get the respect you deserve because you have earned it. You can do it yourself! Your mother gave you life and half your genes. She holds your history, she does not hold your future. Respect her for giving you life, forgive her for what she could not do and claim your own life."

Sometimes I feel like I am talking to the wall as I give my mini-speeches, but once in a while 5 or 10 years later, a young woman will tell me that when I said a particular thing, she remembered it and now she understands what I meant.

I'm from the south and we tend to speak in axioms. We have colorful descriptive phrases for almost every situation. I've tried to tone down my use of these, but they still slip into my conversation. In talking with one young girl about her choice of companions, I told her, "If you lay down with dogs, you get up with fleas." Then years later, she called to tell me that she had made great changes in her life and was living clean and sober, and was getting married to a wonderful man. She said, "Nana, I laid down with dogs and you were right. I got up with fleas. Now I don't associate with people who aren't a positive force for good in my life. I want my daughter to have a real family and a mother who will be there for her."

One of the hardest things for foster children to deal with as teenagers is never having the right clothes. In a society where such great weight is placed on having the latest hot brand names and where participation in any sport is an expensive thing, it's hard on kids who have limited resources. I had a young woman in my home who was an outstanding soccer player. Her shoes, shin guards, uniform and fees were well over $200 and the school no longer provided bus transportation to meets, so I had to transport her to all "away" games. Cheerleading camp and uniforms is $1,000.

There is a foster care support organization in Seattle called Treehouse. They do wonderful things in helping to meet these kinds of needs. The caseworker must request the help and the worker from Treehouse calls the foster parent and finds out what the cost of the needed item is and a check is sent. The problem is often that there is no time. When a kid needs a uniform or shoes and shin guards, it's now, so most foster parents buy these things out of their own pockets and hope maybe to be reimbursed.

Proms have become outrageous in how expensive they are. The tickets are $50 – $100. Add dress, shoes, hair and nails, and you are looking at $300. This needs to change. Whatever happened to dancing in the school gym with parent chaperones, with decorations created by the art class? We have allowed TV to set the standards and the kids think they should have a media event instead of a school dance. This means that students with limited resources can't participate and foster kids can forget it. Is it any wonder that half of foster kids drop out of high school? They can't participate in most of the extracurricular events and these are what keep kids interested in school.

Reader's Digest had a blurb in the July 2005 issue that stated it only costs $6.15 a day to eat meals that meet USDA healthy guidelines. That's $184.50 per month. Add $100 to that for allowances and clothing. There is not much left for such things as prom dresses, hair cuts, perms, sports equipment, makeup, transportation, etc.

We have to do better! Our kids are the future of this country. What is the profit in fighting wars and abandoning our own children to live in poverty? Our job is to give our young people the skills to succeed, but we must also give them the sense of possibility. We must inspire them to believe that they have a future and we must provide a roadmap to that future. We must educate their hearts and minds. We must offer our own lives as examples. Foster children have no role models. They have no moral compass because the family is the provider of those things and when the family fails, they are left without a teacher to show them how to live a productive, moral life. We as foster parents take on that role. We must be examples and we must articulate those values. A work ethic is taught by rewarding work. When a young person is made to feel valued for a job well done, when they receive pay for a job well done, we are hardwiring their brains for productivity. This needs to start at a young age to be most effective. Many of the teens who come into my home have never learned the basic skills to care for themselves and their possessions. It is hard work to teach a 15-year-old how to make a bed, run a vacuum and launder their clothes.

Behavior modification starts with teaching. We must show how we want it done and we must articulate why it needs to be done, and we need to reward the child when it is done. We also need to know the child well enough to discover what rewards the child finds worthwhile. You must listen, observe, question and give the child a sense of empowerment. They need to be able to predict what will happen if they fail to do what is required, and they need to know what will happen when they do what is required.

One of the jobs that kids can do for extra money in my house is cleaning the bathroom. They get $5 for a thorough job. Sometimes a kid will ask to clean the bathroom 10 minutes before they plan to leave for an outing. I explain that would equal $30 an hour and I don't pay for a 10-minute job. I let them know that they can do the job tomorrow when they have 30 minutes to do it right. They know this is fair and they know they need to plan ahead.

One of the things that must be considered in doing foster care is the impact it will have on your own family. My grandson has lived his whole life with foster children. We had to set very strict guidelines when he was a baby and young child. One of our rules was that he was not to be touched, picked up, teased or corrected by the girls. When a child is young, older kids often treat them like toys. They don't respect the little child's boundaries, and many foster kids have been abused and have the potential to be abusive. We made it absolutely clear that they had no responsibility for his care. When he grew to the preschool and kindergarten stage, some of the girls liked to interact with him, but we had a rule that they could only be with him in "line of sight." They could sit on the living room floor and play puzzles or color, or build with Legos if we were in the room. Josh would sometimes get attached to a particular girl and it was hard for him to see them leave. We had to explain to him that he was ours and he would never leave until he grew up. As he got older, he realized that kids went away, but they came back to visit and that they were growing up. Now he is growing up and we have to make sure that he is never left alone with any of the girls, so that there can never be the possibility of allegations of inappropriate conduct on his part. We have an alarm system in the house and his door has an alarm on it. This is for his protection. He is a tall, handsome young man at 15 and he has his own friends and a large support system. He is an honor student and on the swim team. He does not socialize with the girls placed in my home. I have tried to make sure that the girls I take are older than him and that they are never in the same classes at school. This is for his protection. I had one girl placed in my home who very quickly became fixated on him. She would follow him around and sit close to him and constantly try to engage him in conversation. I had her moved because he was uncomfortable and I felt like she had no boundaries. This can be an issue whenever there are teen girls in a home where there are males. Husbands and fathers have to be aware that they need to be always protective of their reputation and that when children have abusive histories, there is always the possibility of allegations being made against them.

We make it a policy not to touch the girls. This may seem extreme, but so many of our kids have been abused sexually or physically that we don't know how they will interpret even a hug. When you have a no touch policy, you have to give caring messages in other ways. You may make a special effort to let kids know they are special. One girl was surprised when I remembered her favorite ice cream flavor and her favorite color for her birthday party, even though she had only mentioned it once. The greatest gift you can give a child is to listen and to let them know they are special.

Amy came to our home from a halfway house after completing drug treatment. Her hair was bright red, "dyed," and while she was in my home it was blue, purple, pink and white. She changed the color regularly and her clothes were "creative" to say the least. She wore lots of plastic bracelets and necklaces, striped socks with combat boots. Somehow she put it all together with style and she was really cute. Amy's mother was mentally ill and was unable to work. She heard voices and had hallucinations. She had been hospitalized several times and was on medication, but sometimes refused to take it. They lived in an 18-ft. travel trailer and Amy's mother sold pot as a way of making a living. Amy had a great sense of responsibility to take care of her mother. She also had a fear that she herself might be schizophrenic because she sometimes knew things before they happened. I talked with her a lot about her mother's illness and about her fear that she was mentally ill. I told her I saw no signs of any kind of thought disorder and that a lot of people had strong intuition, and that hers was probably highly developed because she was always on guard trying to predict what would happen with her mother. She seemed to accept that and to relax a bit. She completed ninth grade and did well at Kamiakin Junior High. During the summer, she began using drugs again. She was going to AA/

NA meetings three times a week, but it was clear to me she was using. I began to encourage her to think about going back in "in-patient" treatment, but she was not receptive.

One evening, Amy failed to return at curfew and I filed a run report. She was gone for about three weeks and was picked up by the police. She was with another runaway child and they had been arrested for shoplifting. I decided to take her back because I felt she really needed someone to "hang in there" with her and she had been with me for a year. We had a bond. She made it through the summer and began 10th grade at Juanita High School. Shortly after school started, Amy was arrested at school for possession and selling drugs. She had 1/2 pound of pot in her backpack. Her mother was arrested on the street outside the school. She admitted that she had brought the drugs to Amy to sell at school and that Amy was selling it on the school campus and giving her the money. Amy was sent to detention and then to a group home. She called now and then to check in and after she was released, she went to San Francisco with her boyfriend. They lived with his parents and Amy entered college where she studied culinary arts. She really liked it and hoped to have a career in the field. She has been clean and sober for almost three years.

I often think of any and her wonderful creativity. She grew up in horrible circumstances without anyone to teach her how to live. She spent her whole youth in survival mode and she did whatever she could to keep herself and her mother fed and alive. What a terrible burden for a child to have to carry. You may ask what did I do to help Amy. I gave her a different vision of herself and how the world works. She had lived her whole life with mental illness as her picture of what was normal. I did not preach or condemn what her mother was doing. She was trying to survive, but Amy was paying too high a price, and when she had a chance to live in an environment that was predictable, she began to see life differently. It was not a straight road for her and she loved her mother. She was able to see another way of life and that she had a chance to reach for something more. I see Amy as a success story even though she had a lot of ups and downs. She saw a future for herself beyond the drug culture and she went for it.

Nicole was not so lucky. She was 16 when she came to my home from California, where she had been living with an older sister. The sister had sent her to Seattle to live with a family friend who had cared for Nicole as a baby. Nicole's father had lived with this woman and together they had parented her when she was a young child. Nicole's father was a fisherman and he had died in a work-related accident when she was 12. The family friend was a cook on a fishing trawler and she spent six months of the year in Alaskan waters at sea. She could not leave Nicole unattended, so she placed her in state custody. She shared some concerns that Nicole was using drugs. My first impression of Nicole was that she seemed younger than her chronological age. She had large round blue eyes, a turned up nose and a bright smile. She was cute and friendly. When I put her in school, she tested below grade level and her records from California showed her having an IQ of 85. After a few days, I could see that Nicole suffered from fetal alcohol or fetal drug effect. She was easily distracted, had no impulse control and could not remember things. We began trying to teach her computer skills and she was a willing student, but she couldn't remember what she had learned from one day to the next.

Nicole stayed for six months and I found myself treating her like a 12-year-old because that was where she was functioning. She got a part-time job at McDonalds and she did okay as long as she stayed on food prep, but she would get confused on the drive-through window. We opened a bank account for her and matched her savings. She had a boyfriend who was three years older and I felt that he was not a good influence on Nicole. One day he and Nicole went to the house of a couple they knew and pulled out a gun and robbed them. I always believed that this was a drug connection and they thought the couple wouldn't report it. That was an error in judgment because they did report it and they knew the names and addresses of both the kids. Nicole was charged and pled guilty to armed robbery and was sent to adult women's prison. She is still there.

In all my years of working with these children, the greatest tragedy I see is drug and alcohol affected kids. They have no real chance of recovery because the damage cannot be healed. They have a lifetime disability and you can't see it, but it colors everything they do. They simply don't have the capacity to handle their lives. They are addicts at birth and if they ever try drugs, even once, they are hooked again. What a terrible legacy to pass on to an innocent child!

Vera was another case of a child born drug affected. She was only 13 when she came to my home. She had been in the custody of an aunt in a small town in Kentucky. She had a twin sister that had remained with the aunt. I don't usually take 13-year-olds because they are too vulnerable to the influences of the older kids, but the social worker was someone I respected and this kid was Irish and Choctaw Indian, which is what my own ethnicity is, so I decided to make an exception. Vera came and she was bright, cheerful and very high energy. She also had severe attention deficit disorder and would forget what she was doing from one minute to the next. She had learned to compensate very well and wrote notes to herself to keep on track. She had a very high IQ and had done well in school. She was also very dramatic. She would come bouncing into the house and announce to the world, "Your favorite foster kid is home!" This did not make her very popular with the other kids in the house. She had fights with her roommates and in the year she was here, I had her change rooms five times. She liked to play the victim and could not accept the fact that she was causing most of the problem. She tried on a different personality every week or two. She went for the Brittney Spears look and tried to sing and dance, but figured out pretty quickly that job was already taken. She decided she would be an intellectual and checked out volumes from the library. She decided she would learn Portuguese and checked out language tapes. She knew nothing about her Choctaw heritage, except the fact that she was registered and we spent hours talking about culture and what it means to be Choctaw. She missed her twin a great deal and would write long letters and have long phone conversations weekly. She also began court-ordered visits with her mother. Vera and her sister had been removed from their custody when they were nine, and she remembered the beatings and lack of food and the alcohol abuse. She had a great deal of stored up resentment. Her mother denied ever having used drugs, but Vera had a copy of the order, which listed the various drugs that were in her mother's urinalysis. She made the statement to me that drugs must be important because her mother and father chose them over her and her twin.

After about nine months, I saw a dramatic change in Vera's behavior. She was more scattered and her grades were falling. Other kids were reporting that they had money missing, and then their clothes began disappearing. On Halloween night, Vera stayed home and was the doorkeeper for handing out candy to the trick-or-treaters. Lisa and Josh had been to a school party and when they returned, Lisa set her purse down next to the candy bowl, then she hung it on the door of her bedroom. The next morning, she found her wallet had been stolen. In it were her credit cards, social security card, her work keys and $70. We did a house search and found the wallet in Vera's room. The $70 was missing, but everything else was still in the wallet. At first, Vera tried to deny taking it, but she was the only one who had real access and she had the wallet in her possession. I grounded Vera for two weeks and gave her 10 work hours to complete. She was allowed to go to school, but nowhere else until she completed her punishment. Just before Christmas, her mental health counselor reported to me that her expensive new cell phone was missing, and she had it last when she was meeting with Vera. About two weeks later, I found the cell phone in Vera's room. Vera had also been losing weight and I had shared my concern that she was using drugs, but by this time, Vera had been assigned a new social worker, who was much less experienced. I asked that Vera be drug tested, but she refused, saying it was an invasion of privacy and she wouldn't do it unless Vera consented to the procedure. At that point, I had done all I could, so I told her to move Vera out of my home. She was placed in a home in a rural area in a small town. About four months later, I got a call from my placement desk asking if I would take Vera back. She had blown out of her placement. I refused. What will happen to Vera? I don't know, but sometimes I have to release a kid to whatever fate they choose, knowing I was unable to do anything. She has been added to my prayer list and I ask God to keep her safe.

I have written a lot about kids and drugs, and I want to make sure that I don't leave the impression that all foster kids use drugs. That is not the case at all. Foster kids are simply more vulnerable to all the negative influences. They want to fit in and the first kids who approach new kids in a new school are the druggies. They offer friendship, but it's really based on drugs. Many foster kids come from homes where drug and alcohol abuse are part of their daily lives. That's what brought them into care. That means that these kids often see substance abuse as normal. If these kids are suffering from FAE or FDE, then first-time of use of either alcohol or drugs, and they are dealing with a full blown addiction.

SuLi was 17 and in 12th grade. She was an honors student with a 3.9 grade average. She had never been in foster care. She had two younger brothers and a younger sister. The school nurse had discovered bruises on the back and thighs of two of her young siblings. She called Child Protection Services and they removed all the kids from the home. SuLi was quite upset because she had been used to taking care of the younger children and she was now separated from them. She had been allowed to go only to school and study. She had never had a date, been to a football game, to the mall or anything that American teens take for granted. She said she hoped to go to college, but her parents would soon be looking for a suitable husband for her. She had been born in Thailand, but her father was Chinese. They came to the states when SuLi was eight years old. She wore thick heavy glasses and was so nearsighted that she could hardly see without them. She was quiet and respectful and very scared. The school year was just starting spring quarter and I did not want her to have to change schools, so I drove her to school in north Seattle for several weeks. She had been so restricted and sheltered that she was operating at a much younger level than her actual age. She lacked practical living skills and judgment. She jumped off a 7-ft. high loading dock and broke her heel plate. She said she didn't know it would hurt her. She dropped a wall mirror on her toe and almost severed her tendon. She was on crutches for several weeks. It became almost a joke among the other kids. What would SuLi do next? SuLi met a young Indian man who worked at the Orange Julius stand and fell in love for the first time. He began to come visit her and take her to movies. I insisted that she must only go out in a group because she was so inexperienced. This went on for several weeks and seemed to be working well. He was respectful and good natured and SuLi was having fun. CPS had begun the process of family visitation to try to reunite the family. They were having family counseling every Friday, and every other weekend SuLi would go home for a weekend visit. She would go to counseling and her home visit directly from school because the counseling center and her home were close to the high school. Then she would return to my home after school on Monday. This pattern went on for several weeks and seemed to be working well. The family was making progress.

One Friday, SuLi packed her weekend bag and got ready to go on her home visit. She left in good spirits and I expected her to return after school on Monday. About noon on Monday, I got a call from the school nurse. She had SuLi in the clinic at school and she was very upset. The school nurse asked me to come to the school and pick her up. When I got there, SuLi confessed to me that she had not gone home because the home visit had been cancelled. Instead, she had gone to Victor's house to spend the weekend. His parents were out of town. She and Victor had had sex, "her first time." She was scared and was afraid she might have gotten pregnant. One of her friends convinced her to go see the school nurse and get the "morning after" pill. She told the nurse that she had been raped because she was afraid that she wouldn't give her the pill if she knew it was her boyfriend. The school nurse had called the police and a report was being filed against the boyfriend for sexual assault. I called the social worker and let him know what had happened. He was very guarded in his speech because he knew he had goofed up big time by not notifying me that the family visit had been cancelled. Everyone started scrambling to cover themselves from any legal liability, and I had a sinking feeling that somehow this incident was going to come back and bite me. I tried to calm SuLi down because she had talked to Victor and told him that the police were involved and he might be charged with sexual assault. He was furious and told SuLi that he didn't want to ever see her again. SuLi decided that she had no choice but to kill herself because she had lost the love of her life and her virginity. I asked her to tell me exactly how the incident had happened. She said they were in bed together and he started to kiss her and to take off her clothes. She said she didn't really want to have sex, but it just happened. I asked her if she had told him to stop. She said no. I asked her if she had tried to push him away. She said no. I asked her why and she said she was just weak. "So you didn't let him know in any way that you didn't want to and you were in his bed with no clothes on? SuLi, he didn't really rape you did he?" She agreed that he had not, but she was afraid of what would happen if her parents found out. She knew they could not find her a husband if she was not a virgin. She wrote long letters to Victor and had friends deliver them, and soon they were talking on the phone again. She decided to live and maybe she would choose her own husband.

SuLi graduated from high school and got a job at a local bank. She began community college in the fall, and CPS returned her and her siblings to her parents. She got her AA degree and decided to study accounting. She is currently pursuing a CPA degree and she and Victor are still dating. He is also in college and has just purchased his first home. SuLi got new modern glasses and contacts. She is very lovely and has developed a lot of poise. I know she will continue to do well.

Andrai was a high-achieving student. She was used to a very comfortable life style. She had entered the system at 16½ because she had bruise marks on her back where she had been beaten with a belt. A teacher had reported it and CPS got involved. Andrai said her mother beat her regularly and called her a slut and a whore. She was a sad little girl who put on a bright smile and tried to pretend that everything was okay. The parents got a lawyer and the state quickly agreed to return Andrai to her home with family counseling. When Andrai was told that she would be returned home, she broke down and began to sob. She kept saying, "I'm afraid to go home. I'm not safe there." The caseworker assured her that she would be okay and that her mother had agreed not to hit her any more. The caseworker felt that with support Andrai would be fine. Family counseling was put in place and everything seemed to be going well. A few months later, I got a call from the caseworker saying Andrai needed placement again. I agreed to take her back. She had a complete breakdown at school and confessed that her father had been sexually abusing her for three years. Her mother knew about it and blamed Andrai for it. She said she was a slut and a whore and that was why her mother beat her. Her father lavished expensive gifts on Andrai and the mother had told Andrai that she would kill her if she told anyone because she had no intention of giving up her lifestyle and living in poverty because she had a tramp for a daughter.

Both the caseworker and I felt bad that we had not listened more closely to that child when she said she was not safe there. We had missed it completely. Everyone had focused on the mother as the abuser and no one even thought to ask about the father. Money talks and once again the big time lawyers were brought in. The father agreed to counseling and community service, and agreed to have Andrai placed out of the home. He also agreed to pay for her college and ongoing counseling. A family who had known Andrai all her life agreed to take guardianship of her so she could finish high school.

I never saw or heard from Andrai again. I hope she has some peace in her life and that she is doing well. We think that incest is something that happens in homes where people are poor and uneducated. It happens in all kinds of environments, rich and poor, uneducated and PhDs. It crosses all social strata and it is devastating to the victim. When the person who is the abuser is also an authority figure in the life of the child, the boundaries are breached and trust is broken. The child will spend a lifetime with trust issues and post-traumatic stress. They will question every relationship and their own judgment. They pay far too high a price because someone who should have been a protector and a role model failed them in the worst way.

One of the issues in working with teens in foster care is the issue of bonding. Teens are at a stage in their development when they are trying to separate. To expect that they will bond with the foster parent in a parent-child type relationship is unrealistic. I have had more success in taking the role of a teacher. "While you are in my home there are some things I can help you with. I want to make sure that you are going to be successful as an adult. There are so many things to learn. You will need to know about banking and renting and how to shop and how to set up a budget. You will need to know about health care and birth control and legal responsibilities. These next few months we will focus on these kinds of things. While you are here I expect you to treat everyone with courtesy and respect. That is how our family works. You will have certain responsibilities within the home that will help to make the house run well. If you need help in learning how to do any of these things, I will teach you. When people live in a group everyone is responsible for making it work. I hope that we will become friends and that this will be a positive experience for you. There are certain things that I must do and some things I cannot do because that is how the state has set up the foster care system. I must provide a clean safe supportive environment. I must report anything that you tell me that will concern your safety. I must report any drugs and alcohol use, any physical violence and any criminal activity. I cannot give permission for you to get piercing, tattoos, take certain classes, have surgery, leave the country or participate in boating, sky diving or other high risk activities. I don't have the legal authority to do so. I want to help you to be successful in school. If you do not attend school, I can be held responsible and I can be fined. This would be true if you were my natural child and it's a very important thing. Your future depends on it, so I put a lot of weight on making sure you get what you need to succeed. A lot of kids who come into my home have some problems with school because it's hard to focus on learning when your life is in crisis. There are special programs to help get kids back on track if they need help. We will work together to find what is best for you. I would like to get to know you and I want to make sure that you are comfortable while you are here. You may be here for a short time or for a very long time and I don't have control of that. Your social worker and the court make placement decisions. I want your time here to be a time when you can relax, take a deep breath and get you life back on track. I can't change what has happened that brought you into foster care. I can try to make your experience here a good one. I hope you enjoy your stay with us. Welcome to our home."

I have made it a policy to have the kids call me "Rita." I find that a lot of kids will switch to calling me "Nana" after they have been here a few months, that's what my grandson calls me, and as they start to bond and feel at home, they begin to use that form of address. That is fine with me and it doesn't set up the loyalty issues that using the title "Mom" does.

Tilly came one evening after being arrested for trying to steal a pair of shoes at the Fred Meyer store. She had been kicked out of her mother's home and had "been on the streets" for a couple of weeks. The weather was cold and wet, her feet had gotten wet and her shoes were falling apart. She was caught in the act of stealing because her own shoes and feet stunk so badly that the clerk was watching her and called security. The security guard called CPS.

I asked her to leave her shoes outside because the odor was overpowering. Tilly was a big girl, about 5' 8" and weighing about 190 lbs. She had long brown hair, blue eyes and a pleasant expression. She seemed to be intelligent and wanted to get off the streets. She told about the hunt every night to find a safe place to sleep and how she was always hungry and always afraid. I sent her downstairs with a change of clothes and told her to take a bath and to shampoo her hair. I gave her clean socks and shower shoes, and told her to come upstairs when she was cleaned up; I would fix her some dinner and we would talk about the house rules. Tilly went downstairs and took a shower and shampooed her hair and returned upstairs. We sat at the table and I began to explain the house rules. While sitting at the table with Tilly, I noticed she still had a very strong and unpleasant body odor. I got her settled in her room and introduced her to her roommate. She was good-natured and seemed to be glad to have a bed to sleep in. The next morning Tilly's roommate asked to switch rooms because the odor was so bad, she said it gagged her. I talked with Tilly about it and tried to be sensitive. Tilly was offended. She could not smell her own body odor. I bought special powder for her feet, but she would not use it. The other girls continued to complain. Tilly would bathe and dress in the bathroom and the bathroom would smell so bad that I would have to spray Lysol on everything before anyone could use it. I took Tilly to a doctor and they pronounced her healthy, except that she had cysts on her ovaries. She was treated for her foot fungus, but still the odor problem persisted. She got a job as a receptionist in a hair salon, but she was let go after two weeks because the customers were complaining about the odor. I finally moved her into a room by herself because no one could or would stay in the room with her. She bathed regularly, she looked clean, but this was a serous problem. The other girls in the house liked Tilly on a personal level. She was sweet and funny and tried to get along. The odor began to permeate the whole house and I could smell it when I walked in my front door. I didn't know what to do with this situation. I was considering having her removed, but I felt bad because I knew she could not help having this problem. I talked with the doctor again and she said that some girls and boys experience this problem when they enter puberty and that Tilly's ovarian cysts may have delayed her onset of puberty, even though she was 17.

Family counseling was put in place and the case worker decided to send Tilly home, with the organization, Home Builders, going into the home to help the family learn new ways of interacting. When Tilly left I had to replace the mattress she has slept on. I did not hear from her for several years. Just recently I saw Tilly again. Lisa and I were out for dinner in a local restaurant when a young woman approached our table and asked if I remembered her. She looked happy and healthy. She had a four-year-old son with her. She and her mother were out together. She told us she was doing well. She was in college and was living in Seattle with her son. She did not have a bad body odor at all. Whatever had caused the problem had been resolved. She did tell us that she had been diagnosed with poly-cystic ovarian syndrome, that she had to struggle to keep her weight down, and had a problem with acne and hair growth on her face. She asked about the other girls who had been in the house while she was there and how she would like to see them.

Her mother refused to come to our table and took her grandson and left the restaurant. She was clearly uncomfortable with Tilly talking with us and wanted no part of us. This is not an uncommon reaction. Parents often resent foster parents. We remind them of a time when they were having trouble with their child and they see it as a failure. Tilly said that she and her mother had developed a great relationship. Clearly this mother had worked hard to rebuild a good relationship. This was not a failure on her part. It was a great success.

I once had a parent show up at my door and bring a gallon of milk with her daughter's name on it because she felt that my limit of two glasses of milk a day was depriving her child. She asked for a written menu of what I fed the kids and wanted me to enforce the same rules in my home that she had in hers. I refused, and told her that she could request the so-cial worker have her child placed somewhere else, but that I would decide how I ran my home. I told her I would not make her child follow different rules, unless it was an issue of health and safety. She called me incompe-tent and said she planned to take my license away and sue me.

One time I had a diamond and sapphire tennis bracelet stolen by a parent. I had gotten dressed to go to a gallery opening for my artwork and decided at the last minute that I didn't like what I was wearing. I quickly changed my blouse and the bracelet didn't match. I pulled it off and placed it on the bathroom counter. I planned to put it away, but the doorbell rang and one of my kid's mother and sister were at the door to pick her up for a visitation. They asked if they could use my bathroom and I said yes. After they took the girl and left, I went into the bathroom and my bracelet was gone. I called the police and they took a report, but said that unless I could prove they had it, I didn't have a prosecutable case.

I also had a parent of a teen in the neighborhood show up at my door and demand to search my house because her daughter was missing and she was sure she was hiding in my house. I talked with her for half an hour at my front door as she threatened me and called me bad names. I never raised my voice, but continued to assure her that her daughter was not at my home and that she would probably show up, and that she should file a police report if she didn't return by late evening. She finally calmed down and left. Lisa asked me why I had been so patient with her as she continued to be abusive to me. I said that she was clearly scared to death about the safety of her child, and the last thing she needed was for me to get into a screaming match with her. She was out of control, but I refused to let her make me act any way that I was not comfortable with. Her child did return home around 11:00 PM and they were able to work out their problems. She never came to me to apologize for her behavior. I think she was embarrassed.

Being a foster parent requires that you be the best possible neighbor. Your kids will be blamed for anything that goes wrong in the neighborhood. You will need to keep your grass cut, your radio down, your pets under control. If the kids are outside, they will be expected to dress in modest fashion, and there will be comments if their skirts are too short or their tops too revealing. If the police show up at your door, which they do at my house on a regular basis because they often have ongoing cases involving the kids, someone in the neighborhood will put a negative connotation to it and gossip will spread about the kids in your house. I had a child go into insulin shock once and I called the aid car. While they were working with the child, I had a neighbor knocking on my door demanding to know "What's going on over here."

Throughout the years I have had good neighbors too. I've had people welcome the kids and make special efforts to get to know them. When we lived on Finn Hill, neighbors took some of my kids to sporting events. They also got the people who worked at Microsoft to donate money to buy a state-of-the-art computer for my girls to use, and they bought all the software programs and tutorials for the girls to learn the computer. They also took two of my kids to a Microsoft picnic. One neighbor, Aleatha, drove one of my kids to Colorado to visit relatives. She was going to Texas and went several hundred miles out of her way to do this. Now that is a good neighbor.

For every insensitive neighbor I come across in this business, I find more who are willing to reach out and help in any way they can. People usually have one of two reactions when they find out what I do. They say, "you must be crazy" or "you must be a saint." Neither is true. I really like kids. I find them interesting and fun to be around. They are growing and changing so fast that you often get to see the transformation. I say it's like seeing the light go on in their brain. Knowing I had a part in that is rewarding for me.

One of my kids, who is now a young adult with two children, is in therapy because she has issues with bonding. She was abandoned at an early age by her mother and lived in several foster homes before being placed with me. She said she gets scared and anxiety ridden when she thinks of being committed to her husband and children for a lifetime. She wants that, but she fears it because, growing up in foster care, she learned that nothing was permanent and, when problems came up, she would get moved, so she never learned about working through issues and how to fix conflicts. She said therapy is helping, but she sees a pattern in her life of leaving things, jobs, relationships, and schools. All can be walked away from, and that's what she has done. She is afraid that, if she gives her whole heart to this man and to her children, she will lose them and she doesn't think she could survive that. We talk a lot on the phone about her feelings of anxiety, and I tell her she will always be a separate individual, but sharing her life with her husband and children is much more rewarding than being alone. She felt so alone for so long that it is familiar, but it's not the best way to live. She is making progress, but it's hard work.

No matter how much we love and care for our foster children, they will deal with these kinds of feelings. If we build a strong bond with these children, that bond must continue long after they grow up and leave the foster home. We become surrogate families. We set the standards for relationships that they will follow in their lives. This is a huge responsibility and should not be taken lightly. Kids who have a family to return to won't need us long-term. There are many kids who have no one they can call family. When they grow up, and many have children, they need and want to feel like someone is there in their background caring about them. One of the things I find happening a lot is the need for young mothers to have a sounding board about parenting. They call me about breast-feeding, colic, sleep problems and toilet training. These are the kinds of questions young women usually go to their mothers with. If there is no mother to go to, there is a large hole in their lives, and they turn to the person who was there for them. They may be 26, 28 or 30, but they still need that general support. Anyone considering becoming a poster parent of teen girls should know that, in many cases, the relationships continue and you become a surrogate grandparent when these young woman grow up and have children.

The key and strength of foster parenting is in the strength of the relationships you build. It is not just about housing, feeding, clothing, and monitoring behavior. It is much deeper and more complex. It is about giving children a sense of being involved and respected and understood. It is about connecting on a separate level. When this happens, real growth and maturity can happen for the child.

When a child has an intact family, we are the bridges over the troubled spots in the life of the family, and they will return to the birth family for their support. This is as it should be. This is what foster parenting is supposed to do. When a child has no family to return to, they see us as their family.

You should see my house on Thanksgiving Day. It sometimes feels like a family reunion, as kids drop by or come for the day and bring their babies for us to see, and they reconnect with other kids they knew while in my home. It's my favorite holiday.

Someone special -

Someone special that is not your mother is willing to care for you. She is loving, caring, strong and understanding. When you are down she will always be there for you. When you are happy she is happy for you. She is not only a mother but she is my best friend. So when it is time to say goodbye, it won't be goodbye it will be, see you later. You are my mother and confidant. Thank you for being there when others couldn't or wouldn't or when I would run and still you took me back. I hope you are around 40 or more years, stay strong and happy.

Love, Alicia

FOSTER PARENTING IS HARD WORK. It can be isolating and frustrating, and there are times when I throw up my hands and want to scream, "What are you thinking?" An example of this is the issue of bus tickets for transportation for the "short-term placement" kids. For years I purchased the tickets and the state would reimburse me when I submitted the receipts. The book of tickets I bought cost $12.50 and contained ten tickets. In the Seattle area, there is a youth fare of $1.25 to ride the bus. Now the state sends me adult tickets that cost $2.50 per ride. That is two times the youth fare in Seattle, and I have to have kids sign for each ticket and send this documentation back to get more tickets. Where is the logic in that!

Sometimes kids are returned to situations that I feel are a setup for the child to be abused again when a parent is unable to cope because of health issues or habits of drug abuse. These are decisions I have no power over and I often don't have complete information to even form an opinion, so I try to let it go and say I'm hopeful for a good outcome. I know that every child wants to be with its biological family. We as foster parents must support that. Sometimes it is not easy.

We read in the papers about the cases when young children are returned to abusive parents and end up getting killed. These are heartbreaking, and everyone wants to make a law that will prevent this kind of thing from ever happening again. The truth is that no law will totally prevent these kinds of tragedies. Human behavior is not always predictable. Social workers are mandated to try to keep the family unit intact. It's always a value judgment as to when the parents are ready to have their child returned. Sometimes they make the wrong call. This can result in a child being injured or killed, and it usually ends the career of the worker who made the decision. When the caseloads are too large and social workers are expected to do more and more, something always gets dropped or overlooked. The buck gets passed.

At this time, the buck is being passed to foster parents. Our compensation for caring for these children is being slashed in half in many cases. If a child with extreme behavior problems and mental health issues gets better for a brief time, our compensation is cut. In other words, if we are skilled at teaching new skills, our payments are cut. These assessments are done every six months and everyone who has ever done behavior modification knows it takes a lot longer than that to effect permanent change. We have the option of leaving the system or accepting this new policy. Many people who are skilled providers are leaving. The state's answer to this is to pay foster home retention workers to try to keep people from leaving. They are also trying to recruit new foster parents to take the place of those who are leaving. That is a good idea because more foster families are needed. I wonder if they are telling them that they will be compensated at about 60% of the actual expenses of raising other people's children. I believe the system needs to go through a complete overhaul. In almost every other developed country that provides foster care, the parent is a government worker. They have the same classification as teachers. They have health care, retirement and vacation time.

Many of the kids who end up in foster care as teens are there because no one is available at home to work with them through the rough spots. Single parents are working sixty-hour weeks and two-parent families are both in the work force. The child has too much alone time and no one is available to parent them. It's pretty lonely to come home to an empty house each day with a list of chores on the refrigerator. Now the state is creating that same situation in the foster homes. We can't afford to stay home and parent these kids because we can't pay basic expenses. We are back to bed and breakfast parenting. It doesn't work.

After twenty-four years of raising other people's children, I am considering not renewing my license. I have two teens that have been with me long-term and I know this will be devastating to them. That's why I have not made the final decision. I keep hoping that I can make this work.

The kids who have been in my home have enriched my life and I know I will miss it terribly. In the first chapter of this book I described why I opened my home. The biggest reason was my need to remain at home and to raise my own family. I have loved working with these kids and I know I have made a huge contribution to their lives. Many other people who do foster care have reasons to work at home. This is real work, it's not charity. It is not easy, but it is worthwhile. I hope that one day foster parents will get the respect they deserve. I hope that one day they will be given health insurance and retirement benefits and the status of state workers. I don't think I will see this day in my lifetime.

Meegan was a tall dark Irish beauty. She had white skin, blue eyes and curly black hair. Her smile could light up a room. She had just turned 16 and her father, who could no longer cope with her wild behavior, had placed her in foster care. Meegan's mother was dying of breast cancer. She had been diagnosed when Meegan was eight years old. She had gone through surgery and chemotherapy and had a remission. She was well for about three years when the cancer reappeared and had spread. She had a second round of chemotherapy and was okay for a while. She had just begun her third series of treatment. Meegan's sister, who was twenty, and her father were the main caregivers.

Meegan had identified herself as the "bad kid". She said no one in her family had any time for her. They just kept telling her she needed to grow up and stop being selfish. Meegan admitted that she got mad at her mother for being sick and that she could hardly remember her mom when she was healthy. She said everyone thought her sister was perfect because she took care of her mom, but that she was often mean to Meegan, calling her names and telling her that she was to blame for her mother getting cancer. Meegan tried to hide her pain by using pot and drinking. She often came home drunk or stoned, and her father finally called Child Welfare Services and asked for an out-of-home placement.

When Meegan came to my house, she settled in quickly and began attending school on a regular basis. She seemed to enjoy the structure and predictability. She finished tenth grade and got a summer job at Dairy Queen. There were one or two times when she came home looking high, but for the most part she obeyed the house rules and got along well with the other girls. She still had some issues with her older sister and would quarrel with her on the phone.

Meegan's mother died in late summer and she had a great deal of sadness about not being at home when her mother passed. When her sister left for college, her father asked Meegan to move back home. She did so, and her father tried to repair their relationship. It was not easy and Meegan would drop by and visit and talk about the counseling they were doing. When Meegan turned eighteen she went to Alaska, and I never heard from her again. I hope that she is well and happy.

There were no happy endings in this family tragedy. Meegan's father did the best he could. Meegan got lost in the process, and the oldest child lost her childhood too. Sometimes life is hard and people do the best they can. I hope this family was able to reconnect and find some peace.

Some kids are just not open to any kind of connection with a foster parent. They suffer from attachment disorder. They have suffered too much loss in their lives to attach. It is still possible to work with these children, but their expectation of a relationship is unrealistic. Structure and consistency are very important. They can and will obey house rules if they believe it is in their best interest to do so. It is important to respect their need for emotional distance. They will be slow to trust and quick to bolt and run. I try to show them kindness and respect while maintaining clear boundaries and expectations. I do not take their pain or feel any guilt about being unable to reach them.

I believe children, and people in general, know what they can handle emotionally, and any bond carries emotional risk. Learning can happen even when there is no bond. Structure and predictability frees energy for learning. Many kids see different ways of life at my house. There is love and peace and acceptance. We live in the moment and share laughter and good times. For many of these kids we become family role models because there has been so much pain in their birth family.

Lumi was rail thin and one of the saddest little girls I have ever worked with. She sat on her bed and read books and tried to avoid interaction with any of the other kids. She had trouble walking up the stairs and she ate very little. I was afraid she had some serious health issues, so I took her to the clinic for a checkup. All of the tests were negative, and the doctor said her problem was deconditioning from lack of exercise. I felt like her spirit had left her and she had no hope. She was a refugee from Africa. She had been raised by her grandmother and had lived in a refugee camp for several years. I got her into an alternative school and began the process of helping her to get her green card. After a few weeks she began to act out with the other girls. She would purposely break their things and she began to steal from the other kids. When she got angry with the other kids, she would pee in their wastebaskets. Needless to say, this behavior only made the other kids more hostile toward her. She was moved from my home into a group home and a few months later she aged out of the system. I know that Lumi was so damaged by her early trauma that she will always have problems. No matter how hard we try, we can't fix these kids. We can only pray for them.

Through the years I have worked with a lot of teens that are pregnant. Some of the kids have chosen to terminate their pregnancy. I have not tried to influence their choice, though I have observed that they often have emotional issues following the termination. I have also observed that at least half of these kids will become pregnant again within a year of the termination. The State of Washington does not have much to offer teens that choose to continue their pregnancy. There are very few homes that will take a teen mother and child. There are agencies that will help if the girls are over eighteen or if she will emancipate and be declared a legal adult. That's not always a good option. She loses all support for herself and her ability to finish school and get any of the Chaffee funds for transitional services. She is stuck in poverty. That's a setup for the teen and for her child. This is an area where we need to do better.

I am currently working with a pregnant teen. She is almost eighteen, but due to deliver before she turns eighteen. She is very good at resource management and she has contacted many of the programs that serve young adults, but there are only two programs for teens under eighteen. Both are currently full, though there is a possibility that one of these programs will have an opening in two months. This puts her close to her due date. If she goes before the court and requests emancipation, she will lose the transitional funds that she is illegible for. That includes first month's rent and deposit, help with household items, scholarships for college and many other support programs. If she emancipates, she can go into the adult program, but she will have to be on welfare. There is now a two-year lifetime limit for aid. This means that if she uses her benefits up now, no matter what happens in the future, she and her child would be ineligible for any help from the welfare system. For a 17-year-old girl with little education and no job skills, that is a setup for failure. What will she do for daycare if she can only make $8 an hour? This young woman is a dependent ward of the state. She has no family support. If the state has custody of a child, they are acting as a parent. It seems to me that the state needs to look at this population more closely and develop more resources to serve them. There are a lot of kids in the system who have these issues.

I had a 16-year-old girl placed in my home a few years ago. She had flown down to Seattle with her three-month-old son on a Med-Evac plane because her son had a birth defect that needed immediate surgery. Staying at the hospital, sleeping in the waiting rooms, she was breast-feeding, as she needed to feed her baby every two hours. She was told that she would be placed with her child when he left the hospital. This did not happen. There was no home available. Her child was placed in a pre-adoptive home in another county. The foster parent was led to believe the child would be free for adoption in the next few months. The mother was given two hours visitation two times weekly. This had to be at DSHS and the foster mother had to bring the child to Seattle by ferry for the visits. They were often late or unable to make the visits at all. There had never been any allegations of abuse by this young mother. The state took custody of her child because she was young and homeless. There was nothing offered to her to support her parenting. This young mother was also determined and fearless in her fight to get her child back. She was able to find a distant relative in another state who offered her and her child shelter. She went before a judge and pled her case and the judge ordered her child released to her. She called me four years later to tell me that she had completed a course in nursing and was now a licensed practical nurse. She had married and was expecting a second child.

The caseworker who was responsible for this case made a judgment, solely on the basis of age, that the young woman could not parent her child. She offered no services. She misled the foster parent who was hoping to adopt the baby. The only good that came out of this was that the foster parent and the young mother became friends and have stayed in contact. This had added another support person to the life of the young mother.

I do not advocate teens becoming parents. It is the most difficult job in the world. Most teens are not ready for the responsibility. I do advocate supporting these young mothers so that they can grow in skills and become good parents. Thirty years ago, teen parents were "sent away" to homes for unwed mothers. They were pressured to give up their babies for adoption. I feel that, in many cases, that is still the best option. I also feel this must be the free and informed choice of the teen parent. They need to be given information. They need to be given the support if they choose to parent.

A lot of people through the years have expressed interest in being a foster parent. They want to know what it's like, what they should be aware of and why. I have been successful with so many kids. I try to give as true a picture as I can. You must have a strong enjoyment of children. You need to work with the age group you like best. For me, it's teens. Most people seem to want to work with young children. You must have a willing spirit and know that you will be challenged. You must accept children as they are, not as you wish they were. You must remember that whatever the child's background is, for them, that is normal. They know nothing else until someone teaches them another way of being. When you accept a foster child into your home, you take on an awesome responsibility. You have an opportunity to influence who that child will become and how they see the world. You can't undo what has happened in their past. You can't "love" them into being different. You teach, educate, support, and when the time comes, you release them.

Children are not grateful. They shouldn't have to be. Gratitude will come when they are grown up and know that they were respected and well cared for in your home. Foster parenting is hard. Your furniture will get damaged, your car may be stolen, and your house will not always be neat and clean. Everyone who thinks you are too hard, too soft, or too demanding will criticize you. You will be "tarred with the same brush" when you read horror stories in the newspaper about abuse of foster children by foster parents. You will be accused of "doing it for the money" by the kids and by the people who think foster parents are paid a lot. You will have to deal with a system that does not support you. You will be asked to do much more with less and less.

Are you still interested? If at this point you are, I would refer you to the Department of Licensed Resources. You will be investigated. You will be required to take several weeks of training. You must have personal references and your home will be inspected to see if it meets state requirements. When most people hear this they say, "No thanks." A few hearty souls will still be interested.

When people ask me why I do it, and have done it for so many years, I say, "Because I like it. I like the kids. I like knowing I have helped someone. I like knowing I have made a difference. I am part of a solution. My life has been well spent. I was lucky enough to find something that I was good at and that I enjoy doing year after year. I have not burned out, grown tired of the kids or felt that I needed something different. I have grown frustrated with the state system. I have felt that people who make decisions that impact me have no concept of what the fallout will be. They are looking at paper and money. I am looking at the eyes of children. Our view is different."

I'm now dealing with the impact of the latest change. In the past, the duration of specialized receiving care has been 90 days. It is now 15 days with one possible addition of 15 days. This was a cost-cutting measure. I now have 14-year-old and 16-year-old girls who cannot be enrolled in school. The kids were placed three days ago from "out of county" and have no school records. They have been requested. I can't enroll them until they arrive. The school will not take them because they are too "short stay" to receive any credits. I can't get-well child exams for these kids because the health clinic puts the well child exam at a lower priority then sick patients. It takes two to three weeks to schedule. I don't have immunization records, so I don't know if they need immunizations. The placing caseworker called today to tell me the case had been transferred to a new social worker that would be contacting me within 48 hours. So now we have burned five of the allotted 15 days. Can the new social worker manage to meet these kids, study the case, interview people and go to court, etc., in the next ten days? I don't think so. Can she find a home for a sibling group of four, in that time? The kids are still not in school. In the best of worlds, these girls will find a permanent home quickly, but they will be six weeks behind in school. They will lose credit for the fist semester of school. They will not be able to make up the lost time. Try going into Algebra 1 after missing the first six weeks. Try going into science class after missing the first six weeks. The likelihood is that these kids will lose at least a half-year of credits. If they remain in care until they graduate, they will need care longer to make up for that half-year of school they missed. From my perspective, that is penny-wise and pound-foolish. If we still had 90 days to find permanent placement, I could get the kids in school. The difference in cost to keep a kid in receiving care 60 more days is about $600 more. The cost to provide an extra half-year of care to make up for the lost schooling is about $3,500. This is only the cost of foster care. It does not factor in the social worker's salary to manage a case an extra six months. Pay now or pay later.

The other down side to this new directive is that it does not give placement coordinators a chance to look for a good match. They will place kids in any available home because they have no time to find a home that is a good fit. This is often a setup for the kids. Some people work really well with certain kids and not so well with others. I work very well with "oppositional-defiant" kids. I like kids who are bright and who question authority. I do not work well with kids who are developmentally-disabled or low functioning. I lose patience with them. I know this about myself and will not be talked into taking kids with these challenges, they deserve someone who will work well with them. I have learned to be very selective about the kids I receive into my home. I take kids that I feel will benefit from what I have to offer. They are often kids other people might turn down. One of my long-term kids that is currently in my home had been asked to leave her last four placements. She has done very well here. When I work with a young woman who is oppositional, I try to find out what they really want and what they are fighting against. I try to help them define some goals and do everything in my power to help them reach that goal. I try to make clear what my expectations are and why I have them. Every house rule has a reason behind it and I can articulate the reason for every rule. My belief is that if you have about ten house rules and good reasons for them, kids are very willing to comply. If you have 30 rules, they are always in trouble because they cannot remember all of them. I have tried many things over the years, and I discarded a lot of them.

House Rules:

1. To stay here, you must live peacefully. No fighting, no hitting, no horseplay. If there is a problem, I need to know about it and it is my job to help resolve it.

2. Make your bed and keep your clothing picked up and put away. You may do your laundry as needed, but not after 9:00 at night. Take short showers.

3. Do not lend and borrow clothing. If you ignore this rule, you may lose your clothing and I will not be responsible for it. You must keep up with your own things. Say no! You can say I told you not to lend.

4. I must know where you are at all times. You are allowed to go out for activities and to visit friends, but we must discuss it and I need addresses and phone numbers when you visit friends.

5. Curfew is 8:00 PM on Sunday through Thursday. It is 10:00 PM on Friday and Saturday. This is negotiable for special events. You must ask ahead of time. I cannot okay overnights with friends. This must be approved by your social worker. If you are late, you will be grounded. If you are going to be late, call me on my phone, not the girls' line. If you are late and do not call, I will file a runaway report with the police. You may lose your bed here.

6. You cannot cook on the stove. You may use the microwave oven and the toaster. You must eat at the table, no food is to be eaten in your room. You may have fruit or a sandwich if you are hungry, but not after 9:00 PM. You can have cereal and juice or toaster waffles and toast for breakfast, but you must always clean up what you take out. Don't leave milk or juice or cereal on the counter or table.

7. No drugs and no alcohol use while you are in my home. If you bring these things in, you will be charged with a crime. If you come home impaired, you will be grounded.

8. Do not steal! Do not shoplift, and if you bring anything new into the house, you will be asked for a receipt.

9. My room, Lisa's room and Josh's room and the garage are off limits. You cannot go into those spaces. Do not use my phone.

10. Do not open your windows and do not turn the heat up or down. There is an alarm in the house and you will set off the alarm. If you are too hot in your room, close your heater vent and open your door. Leave the bathroom and laundry room door open when they are not in use.

One of the things I tried and gave up on was color-coordinating everything. One kid would have blue sheets, towels, washcloths and comforters. Another kid would have pink or green. They had to turn in their dirty towel to get a clean one. Their bedding had to be changed at least once a week, etc. It sounded like a good idea, but it became more work for me than it was worth. It felt more like a rule for a group home. I gave up on that one. Now the rule is put your dirty towels in the laundry basket, get clean ones out of the linen closet. I buy a lot of white towels and washcloths. They can be bleached. Another thing I gave up on was rotating kitchen duty. I found that I had to go behind and redo most of what the kids did. Now I make the kitchen a bid job for extra allowance and the job must be done to my standards or they don't get paid. I also have a standard rule, if you use it, put it away. The kids are allowed to get snacks or make sandwiches, but they must leave the kitchen clean, no breadcrumbs on the counter, no peanut butter knife left on the counter. This one takes pretty constant monitoring. I don't make a big fuss about it. I just call the kid back into the kitchen and tell them what they need to do. I say, "I see you forgot to put away your things in the kitchen, could you please come do it now?" This is usually all it takes and they respond well. A lot of kids have never had any structure in their lives, especially if they come from a home where there is alcohol or drug abuse. These kids must be taught the most basic skills of cleaning and taking care of their clothes.

If a person in contemplating taking teens into their home, I would strongly suggest you get an alarm system installed. Teens will sneak out the windows after curfew, they will sneak boys into the house after curfew. They will try to smoke by putting holes in the window screens and holding the cigarette out the window. You will also need locks on your bedroom door and your biological child's door. You will need an alarm on those doors too. You are required to have all medications locked up and I find a fireproof document safe works well for that. You will need to keep all records locked up and, when a child leaves your home, the records need to be shredded or returned to the social worker.

I have found that keeping a daily log is helpful. I list who is in the home each day, any problems or issues the kids are experiencing, contacts with social workers, what was discussed, doctors appointments, etc. I also list dates kids are placed and when they leave. When a kid leaves, I write a short profile, just a paragraph or two about the kid. This helps me a lot. When a kid is placed with me, I do a sheet that lists physical description, allergies, medication, contact persons, legal status and any other information I think may be important. All this should be on the intake form, but is usually not. If you have to file a run report, you will need all this information; don't assume it's on the intake form. You will be asked for hair color, eye color, skin tone, visible scars and marks, tattoos and piercing. This information is not on the intake form. You will also be asked what the child is wearing. You will also be asked if the child has a history of drug or alcohol use and if there is a history of prostitution. You will be asked about medication and mental health. You will be asked if you know the name and phone number of the parents. You will be asked if you know the name of the social worker and/or probation officer. You will be asked if you know the name of the child's dentist. You will be given a case number and you must report this to the social worker. If the child returns, you will need to cancel the run report and you will need the case number to do that. This is one of the reasons I keep a notebook of information that I think I might need.

I also think it is a good practice to do an inventory of the child's possessions when they enter your home. I have found many things in a child's possession that are not okay to have in a receiving home. The most common thing is a knife. I have found switchblades, hunting knives and every possible kind of pocketknife. I have found a stun gun, mace, dog chains with attached locks. These are all potential weapons and must be taken away. I have also found drugs and drug paraphernalia, pipes, bongs etc. I have also heard every possible story about why they are carrying these items: "I have to have protection on the street." "A gang is after me." "I'm holding it for someone else." These things must be reported to the social worker, and if it's drugs, you must file a police report. The teen will be charged with minor-in-possession. You should also be on the lookout for prescription drugs of any kind and over-the-counter medication. No dosage information and cold medications are a big red flag.

Often when a kid is using methamphetamines or crack cocaine, they will use whatever stimulant drug they can get to ease their withdrawal. Keep your awareness on the kid's physical look, condition and physical movements. One of the clues is what I call the crack itch. If a child has been using crack or meth, they develop skin problems as these substances try to clear the system. Kids will cross their arms and scratch their forearms, or they will sit and scratch their upper thighs. They are often completely unaware of these movements, but it is a dead giveaway that they have been using drugs. The only other reason for that is the kid has scabies. Either way, you want to know.

Another issue you may deal with is eating disorders, and this is very complex. We, as foster parents, are not qualified to treat eating disorders, so if you suspect a child has bulimia or anorexia, you need to have her evaluated and work with a therapist that is good with these issues. One of the things I pay attention to is a child who does not want to come to the table with everyone else. They will have many different excuses. "I ate at a friend's house." "I'm not hungry." "I have a headache, I will eat later." Another thing I pay attention to is the kid that always goes to the bathroom immediately after eating. Bulimic kids can vomit without making a sound. If a child has a lot of cavities, you need to pay attention. If a child drinks huge amounts of diet pop, watch for signs of eating disorders. Sometimes I just ask, "I've seen some signs that make me wonder if you are dealing with an eating disorder. Do you need some help with this issue?" Sometimes they will say, "Yes I need some help." At this point, do not tell a child they shouldn't be doing this. Do not blame or shame them in any way. I say, "I'm glad you told me and I will do everything I can to find a person you are comfortable with who can help you. It's really hard to try to deal with this alone." Let the therapist set the guidelines about what, when and how much the child needs to eat. Many times the child feels a great sense of relief that her secret is out and someone is willing to try to help.

You my also deal with a teen who is pregnant and trying to hide it. There are many reasons why. They are frightened and ashamed. They are afraid that they will be kicked out. They are afraid that people will put pressure on them to have an abortion or they are afraid they might be prevented from having one. When you take the child in for her well child exam, it is a good time to talk about this issue. I just come right to the point and ask, "Are you pregnant?" If they say no and I think they are, I say, "I have seen some signs that make me think you might be and I want to help you if you are. When was your last period?" That's usually enough to get the child to tell you if she is. Let her know that she has the right to make decisions about her life and her own body, but that there are people who can help her. In dealing with pregnant teens, I have been asked by several of them what I think they should do. I do not tell them what I think is right or wrong. I try to give as much information as I can and tell them that none of the choices are easy. I will honor whatever choice they make and help them get in contact with people who can help them. My beliefs are not the issue. Their beliefs are what they must deal with.

In an earlier chapter I told the story of Jessa, one of the four girls who were placed together when we lived on Finn Hill. During the time I have been writing this book, I have reconnected with Jessa and I'm glad to share the update. Jessa went to California where she is residing in a "clean and sober" house for recovering addicts. She has been off all drugs for almost a year. She no longer hears voices and has a full-time job. She reports that she is lonely and would like to be in a relationship, but hasn't found anyone to fill some of the lonely places in her life. She has seen her son and she is considering moving to Oregon to be closer to him. She has an open adoption agreement and she is allowed four visits a year. She reports that he is doing well and that his adoptive parents are great people.

Lauren and her daughter, Rayleen, have also reconnected with us. Lauren has met a young man who is in the navy and they are getting married. She has asked me to help her plan the wedding. She has gone through a very hard time in the last two years. Her depression had become completely unmanageable and she was hospitalized. After she got out of the hospital, she asked her mother to leave and find her own place. This took a lot of courage, but it really needed to happen. Rayleen is four-and-a-half and entering preschool. She is a happy, healthy little girl and seems well adjusted and well mannered. I really like the young man Lauren plans to marry. He seems to love her and Rayleen a lot. There are some happy endings and new beginnings.

There are many girls who have lived in my home that I have bonded with in a special way. Some of them are not mentioned in this book. Throughout the years there have been many children who came to my home and stayed a short time. They remain small stories in my memory. I want to mention them because they are illustrations of the pain, suffering, and courage of these children.

Tessa was 14, with curly brown hair and large dark eyes. She was very nearsighted and wore glasses that magnified her beautiful eyes. The result of this gave a quality of shyness and fragility that reminded me of a young deer. She also had about her a watchfulness and a sense of unsureness. My instinct was to put my arms around her and protect her from what it was that she feared. My training told me that was not a good idea. I tried to engage her comfortably. She was waiting for a permanent placement with a relative and I knew she would only be with me a few days. Noting that her glasses were old and scratched, I told her I would make an appointment to get her new glasses. A look of complete terror crossed her face and she asked in a whisper, "Will they put drops in my eyes"? I told her they would and she began to sob and beg me not to make her go. Her reaction was so out of proportion to the situation that I was shocked. I tried to calm her down and told her I would not make her go if she did not want to go. I began to question her about what had upset her and she told me a story about how her mother would punish her when she was bad. If she left her shoes in the living room or forgot to make her bed or any other small infraction, her mother would hold her down and drop vinegar into her eyes with an eyedropper. I was horrified and almost speechless. A few days later, she left my home to go live with a relative. I never saw her again, but I will never forget her.

Marty was 16. She was a tall pretty redhead with beautiful skin and green eyes. She began every sentence with, "I'm sorry." She would get down on the floor and crawl if she had to pass in front of the television when someone was watching it. She had the worst self-image I have ever seen. She had been abandoned by her mother and abused by her grandmother, and then raped by an uncle. After a few days of observing her actions, I sat down with her and told her we were going to change some behaviors that weren't working for her very well. I told her she had a right to be here and she had a given right to live, and she was never ever to get on the floor and crawl again for anyone. I told her she was unique and beautiful and there was no one else in the world like her. I told her it was her duty to hold her head up and claim her place in life, and that she was never to apologize for her thoughts or what she wanted to say again. I made her look in the mirror and say, "I love myself and I am beautiful just the way I am." She was to do this 10 times every morning and 10 times every night. This was hard for Marty at first, but soon she got into it and the change was dramatic. She went to a long-term foster home, finished high school, and started college. About five years later she dropped by to see me. She was poised and well dressed, and she thanked me for helping her. She said I changed her life and that she still made herself look in the mirror and say, "I love myself just the way I am and I am beautiful," and she was!

Rachel was three months pregnant and 14 years old. Her mother was insisting she have an abortion; Rachel was refusing. Her father was in the military service and had been killed about a year earlier. Rachel felt her mother was dishonoring her father's memory because she had begun to date again and didn't want to be responsible for a grandchild. The father of the baby was 16 years old and in no position to support her, even though he was trying. I took Rachel to a doctor to check on the status of her pregnancy, and the doctor was fearful that Rachel had some problems. They did an ultrasound and wanted further testing. We went back to the hospital the following day and Rachel's boyfriend met us there. The test did not reveal any problems, but Rachel's mother became so concerned, she decided to take her daughter home and, with counseling, the family was able to work through their problems. Rachel gave birth to a healthy baby boy.

Kelli Ann was 14 years old and she was ill when the caseworker dropped her off at my house. She had a bladder infection and bronchitis. For which the caseworker left me two kinds of antibiotics. She also left a social summary that said Kelli Ann was placed in foster care because of ongoing conflict with her stepfather. Kelli Ann had a good relationship with her mother, but she felt that her stepfather was demanding and unreasonable. The mother refused to buy into Kelli Ann's manipulations and had placed her daughter in foster care to give the family a cooling off period while they secured counseling for the family. I put Kelli Ann to bed because it was clear that she was quite ill. The placement coordinator had not told me that the child was so ill. About two hours later, I gave her the meds the doctor had prescribed. An hour later, I could see that Kelli Ann was getting worse, her temperature had climbed to 103.5 degrees F. and she was nauseous. I gave her Tylenol and her fever came down, but when

I gave her the next dose of antibiotics, her fever spiked again. The poor child was desperately sick and she just lay in the bed and cried, "I want my mommy." After about six hours of this, I was getting pretty worried. I tried to reach the social worker, but she had gone home for the day. I tried to reach the doctor who had seen Kelli Ann, but was unable to reach him, so I called Kelli Ann's mother. She came right away and we took Kelli Ann to the hospital. They kept her for three days and determined that she was allergic to the sulfa that had been prescribed for her infection and the spiking fever was caused by the medication. This was a high-drama start to a long stay that was punctuated with one crisis after another.

Kelli Ann was small, blond, cute and charming, and she was clearly used to having her way in everything. She wore very provocative clothing and she was able to convince her mother that she should buy her designer-label jeans and underwear. Her underpants cost $45 a pair. Her pushup bras were $150 each. I was aghast at such extravagance and asked the mother to limit the clothing she brought to my house because I could not guarantee it would not be stolen. Kelli Ann started eighth grade and she made it one week before I was called to pick her up from school. She had been suspended for fighting. Over the next month, Kelli Ann was suspended three times. She fought with classmates, she was verbally aggressive with the teachers, and she broke things, slammed doors and generally disrupted class to the point that Eckstein Middle School refused to allow her to attend there. She was placed in an alternative school run by North Seattle Youth Services, and she lasted there about a month.

The interesting thing was that Kelli Ann did not act out in my home or other settings. She had a true school phobia. She was so afraid of the school setting, she would do anything to escape it. She was also becoming depressed, as her mother continued to refuse to leave her husband and, with the counselor's help, she was learning to set limits with Kelli Ann. She had begun to scratch her arms with sharp objects and to talk about just disappearing. One evening she got into an argument with another girl in my home and she left without permission. I was very worried because she left without her purse and her makeup. For me, that was a big red flag because Kelli Ann did not want anyone to see her without her makeup on. I called the police and let them know that I felt this child was at high risk of suicide. We began scouring the neighborhood, and I could feel the panic rising in my chest as the minutes ticked by without finding Kelli Ann. Finally, she was located at a local school, crouched down behind some stairs. At that time everyone agreed that Kelli Ann was in danger and she was placed in Fairfax Hospital in the Adolescent Mental Health Unit. I visited her there several times and she seemed to be responding well to the meds she was on for depression. She came back to my home after being released from the hospital and the Seattle School District refused to let her enter any school in the district, except Wilson Pacific. This was a school that served developmentally delayed students. Kelli Ann agreed to try it and she actually did well there. Kelli Ann was learning disabled and, for the first time in her life, she felt able to keep up. She actually began to look forward to school. She was able to help others and her teachers relied on Kelli Ann to help them with grading papers and doing charts for the developmentally delayed students. With intensive family counseling, Kelli Ann returned to her home and she continued to do well. She attended Wilson Pacific School for one full year and then was mainstreamed into high school.

Wilson Pacific School is no longer in existence. I wonder where the population that was served there goes to school now? Are these the kids in the special education rooms in the regular high schools? Does this work better? I don't know. Wilson Pacific School saved this child and she benefited greatly from being there. She was able to return home and continued to do well. She is now a mother with teenagers of her own.

Terri was adopted when she was two and her adoptive mother was a woman in her mid fifties. She was devoted to Terri and had been involved in her therapy from the time she was in grade school. Terri was a drug-affected baby with ADD and ADHD. She had problems in school and with peer relationships. She had several arrests for shoplifting and two charges for breaking and entering. She had very little impulse control and was easily talked into things. She had a boyfriend who was an Alaskan Indian, who worked as a carver and spent a lot of time hanging out in Seattle on First Avenue with the homeless and street people. Terri's mother felt she could no longer control her daughter, so she asked for help from DSHS. Terri was placed with me while she waited for a group home placement. She did relatively well in my home and she responded well to the structure, but on two occasions she was caught sneaking out after curfew. After she was placed in a group home, I found several blankets under my house and I realized that her boyfriend had been sleeping there.

Terri did well in the group home and was learning to manage her impulsiveness. She became pregnant at 17 and her mother helped her to get an apartment and get a part-time job. She let her boyfriend move in with her. After Terri had her baby, she got a full-time job and things were going well. She had a 16-year-old girl who did babysitting for her. She left the baby with her boyfriend every day for about two hours before the sitter came. One day the babysitter came and the boyfriend left, saying the baby wasn't feeling well and was taking a nap. She went to check on the baby and found him blue and hardly breathing. She called the aid car and the baby was rushed to the hospital where it was determined that the child had suffered severe brain damage from being shaken. The baby did live, but was left permanently disabled and will need supportive care for the rest of his life. The boyfriend left Washington State and returned to Alaska. I don't know what charges were ever filed, but I know that Terri was trying to do things right and take care of her child in spite of her own challenges. Sometimes life is just hard.

Geita was a star! I felt her presence when she walked in my front door. She was six feet tall and very pretty with light brown hair and blue eyes. She was dressed conservatively and spoke in a polite manner. She was almost 18 and her social worker explained her situation. She needed temporary care while she searched for a living situation that she could afford. Her mother had kicked her out because Geita had refused to continue to participate in her mother's ministry to the homeless. Geita's mother believed she had been called to preach and she went to homeless shelters where she held religious services. For years she had taken Geita with her and Geita sang and played various musical instruments. Geita wanted to play jazz music and mom felt that was not God's plan. She told her daughter to give up jazz or leave. Geita left.

Geita had a band and they played at various clubs and restaurants in the area. She came home one day with her brown hair bleached white blond. She walked in with a wary expression on her face and I think she expected me to say something critical about her hair. I told her it was absolutely beautiful and it was! She was stunning, and I'm sure it was perfect for her stage presence. She found a house-share situation and moved out. I heard that she had released a CD, but I never found out what it was or who released it. I still look for her face on TV and hope some day that she makes it big!

The thing that has worked best for me all these years is keeping things simple and predictable. Kids need to know what to expect in the home. They need predictability because their lives are out of control, and so much energy goes into trying to gain some control that they have little energy left for schoolwork or personal growth. They should not have to be worried about routines in the home. Keep it simple, keep it safe, and keep it predictable. Even introducing a new food can be hard with foster kids. If it is something they have never tried, or maybe never even seen, they will quite likely reject it, unless you do some talking about it before it is presented at the table. I recently served polenta and I explained before the meal that I was cooking an Italian dish that was served in Italy frequently. I told them that the sauce was the same one I used with pasta, but polenta was made with corn. They were slow to try it, but they did and all agreed it wasn't too bad. I don't buy a lot of junk food and I always have fruit available, but many of the kids that come to my home have been raised on sweet cereal, potato chips and cookies. The lack of sugar and chips and soda pop are the things they complain about. I offer them juice, milk and fruit instead. I still find it hard to get the kids to accept whole wheat bread and I compromise on that issue and buy white bread for them. I do find that after kids have been in my home for a few months, they will try whole wheat. Small changes add up over time.

Louisa was 16 when she came to my home the first time. She was 5'4" and weighed 250 lbs. She was very proud of the fact that she had recently lost 50 lbs. She had beautiful hair and large brown eyes and a smile that lit up her face and revealed white even teeth. She had attempted suicide and had a history of drug and alcohol use. She was in a high school for troubled teens. Louisa and her mother were in constant conflict and Louisa spent about half of her life living with her aged grandparents. Louisa's mother did not work; she lived on Social Security checks that she received because Louisa's father had died when she was eight years old. Louisa's mother claimed to have lupus and several other health problems. She took large amounts of pain meds and Louisa talked about the many moves they had made because her mother did not pay the rent. They bounced between various apartments and the grandparents' house. Louisa's mother would tell whatever story she thought would gain sympathy and she expected Louisa to take care of her when she was ill or drunk or stoned on pain pills. She controlled her daughter by verbal abuse and told her she was fat and ugly and no one would ever want her. The one bright spot in Louisa's life was her grandfather. He dearly adored Louisa and he tried to protect her from her mother's abuse. He had a home in a good neighborhood and substantial financial resources. Louisa's mother was afraid to cross him because he controlled the money. Louisa had severe asthma and she complained that she could not breathe in her mother's home because of the smoke. Family counseling was tried and abandoned because the mother was so abusive in the sessions that the social worker felt it was too damaging for the teen.

Louisa did well in my home and I could see her depression getting better. She was very social and her grades improved as she had more energy to focus on her studies. Louisa had been with me about three months when she got a bad cold, which quickly turned into asthma. One day at school she was having breathing problems and the mother picked her up from school and took her to the doctor. She called and told me that she was keeping Louisa for the weekend because she was quite ill. I called the social worker and was told that the mother had a legal right to do that because the child was placed with a consent order that the mother had signed, and she still had all her legal rights as a parent. I got a call later that evening from Louisa telling me she was being admitted to the hospital for heart-related problems. The mother had given Louisa three times the prescribed dosage of her asthma meds and Louisa was in danger of heart failure because of the overdose. The mother claimed the meds were incorrectly labeled. When Louisa was released from the hospital, her mother took her home and cancelled her legal consent for placement.

About nine months later, I got a call from the social worker asking if I would take Louisa back into my home. She had called the social worker and requested out of home placement because the abuse had gotten so bad that she could not live with it any longer. Louisa went to court and filed a petition requesting "out of home" placement. When she came to my home the second time, she had gained back all the weight she had lost and about 50 lb more. She now weighed 350 lb. She could hardly walk up my stairs and she had great difficulty walking the block from my house to catch the school bus.

Louisa had a huge circle of friends and though she was morbidly obese, she always had a boyfriend. Part of that I attribute to her personality. She had a way of making people happy, and I never heard her make a cutting or nasty remark about anyone. Louisa stayed with me until she turned 18 and she received about $10,000 from an insurance settlement her father had left her. She got an apartment and various friends asked for loans, which she gave them. Her boyfriend at the time asked her to buy him a car and she did. Within six months, her money was gone and so were her friends. Her grandfather died and her mother took over the management of his estate. She paid Louisa's apartment rent and did whatever she could to make Louisa totally dependent on her for support. Louisa got pregnant and she married the young man who was the father of her child. He was working, but did not make enough money to support the two of them, so they accepted Louisa's mother's offer to move into the home that had belonged to Louisa's grandfather. She now had her daughter back in a totally dependent situation.

Louisa had a difficult pregnancy and was put on bedrest at five months' gestation. Her son was born healthy and beautiful, and the mother took over much of the care of the baby. She criticized Louisa constantly and had her believing she was not capable of parenting her own child. Louisa's mother announced one day that she was selling the house and moving to California. She wanted to go somewhere warm and she was tired of the Northwest. The house sold quickly and Louisa, her husband and son moved with the mother to California.

Louisa called about once a month to tell me what was happening in her life. The mother could not find a doctor who was willing to supply her with the pain pills she was taking and she became more hostile and abusive as she withdrew from the drugs. Louisa's husband left and returned to Seattle and filed for divorce. One day Louisa finally reached her limit. She left her mother's home and went to a shelter. She found a job, got an apartment and has cut all ties with her mother. She reports that she is very happy now and that she is realizing that she is smart and capable and a good parent. She is in a new relationship with a man who treats her and her son well. She has lost 100 lbs. and says she hopes to lose 100 more over the next two years. She says that it took years for her to get the courage to cut all ties with her mother, but when she did she became a whole person for the first time in her life.

Some relationships are so toxic the only way to survive is to leave. Louisa still checks in regularly and gives me updates on her progress. I am proud of her because I know it took great courage to make that leap of faith and leave her abuser behind.

There have been several kids that I have had removed from my home and it was usually because they were unwilling to comply with house rules. Sometimes I moved a kid because they posed a threat to the family. I had one 13-year-old girl placed with me who had been placed with her grandmother and the grandmother reported that the child was sneaking out at night and out of her control. She had been with me about a week and had failed to come home from school on time twice. She was sitting in my living room watching TV when my 28-year-old son came by for a visit. I walked out of the room for about five minutes and my son quickly followed me. He said, "Don't ever leave me alone with that child. Do you know what she just said to me?" This girl had said, "I really like older men. They can f___ you all night. Boys my age lose it in five minutes." I determined that she was too great a risk to remain in my home, so I asked that she be placed somewhere else.

Another kid I removed had failed several previous placements because of aggressive behavior toward peers. She was having some conflict with the other girls, but I was trying to work with her. She came home two hours late and when she came in, I asked her if she didn't understand the curfew or did she have trouble reading the bus schedules. Her reply was, "Don't talk to me about no f___ing bus schedules, I come home when I'm ready to." I said, "Not in my house you don't, go pack your clothes." I went down stairs to monitor her while she was packing and I talked with her about what she was doing. I told her the game she was playing was not working for her and that no one would put up with that behavior. She actually grinned and said, "Most people just let me get away with it." She asked twice after that if she could return to my home. I declined.

One of the hardest things is having a kid removed that has been here long-term and that we have bonded with. I had to do that with one child who had been here for three years. She was almost 18 and had done reasonably well, but she had resumed using drugs and she was bringing them into the home. She was moved to a facility where she was drug-tested weekly and she did clean up, but when she turned 18, she left the system and continued to use. She stopped by to visit a couple of times and she admitted she was still using, but she felt she was okay because it was just recreational. I haven't heard from her in over a year.

I had another child removed because she was clearly fixated on my grandson. She followed him around, sat too close to him and made him very uncomfortable. She also wrote notes that I felt were not appropriate, and my gut feeling was that she was a danger because I was afraid she would lie and say that Josh had made advances or something. My policy has always been to never leave Josh alone with the girls, but that does not protect him from their fantasy lives and their lies if they choose to go in that direction. Anyone who does foster care for teens must always be aware of the risk of allegations against any family member.

When I was a supervisor at the YMCA Crisis Residential Center, we had a young woman make allegations against a staff member. He was a student at the University of Washington in the masters program for social workers. He was professional and a real asset to our program. He was also young, handsome and friendly. The teen told some of the other kids that he had come into her room and kissed her, and told her she was beautiful. We all knew these were false allegations because the staff person never

ever went into a female's room, he never went to the kitchen with one of the female clients, and he never put himself in any position where he might be vulnerable. Still, he was put on paid leave and a police report was filed. The teen admitted under questioning that she had lied because she thought he was cute and she wanted the other kids to think he liked her. She was charged with making a false report and his name was cleared, but he quit the shelter as soon as his name was cleared because he had spent five years of higher education to work in the field of social work and one such allegation could end his career before it was even started. We lost a really good youth worker. He did become a social worker and I think he is now an area manager in another region. I'll bet he is still very careful about being alone with a teen female.

We, as foster parents, are often asked to deal with children whose behaviors are extreme. Many of these kids have burned out their parents, grandparents and other relative caregivers. Many of these children have been brain-injured and were born with problems from drug or alcohol use by the parent or just by a genetic roll of the dice. There are many, many causes for antisocial behavior and we are not miracle workers. We may have years of experience, but we cannot fix some of the issues we are asked to deal with. I will stress again that foster parenting is a job, not a volunteer position. We deserve to be compensated when we take on the responsibility of dealing with these children with acting-out behaviors. We cannot work outside the home and do it right. To ask that of providers is shortsighted, unrealistic and unfair. These children need constant supervision and someone available to be their advocate at school, at home, with the medical and dental offices that treat them. It is not an "after 5" position. When a kid is in a crisis, it is immediate. It is not something we can schedule for after work.

I wonder which administrator or area manager would take any of the kids I deal with into their home. Would they leave them unsupervised while they were at work? I don't think so! Yet, we are now being asked to do just that. We are being told that this isn't a real job and we aren't supposed to be paid to do it. We are expected to take all the risk, all the damage, all the hard work, and all the heartbreak for less money than we could rent the room for to an adult. The only reason anyone would do foster care under these current circumstances is because they believe in the possibility that these children can be helped and they want to be a part of that. You cannot pay for that, but we should be paid for our time and our skill. If the Children's Administration wants "a good outcome," it is time to get real about the cost of providing care for the state's dependent children.

I have a young mother and infant child in my home now. I don't usually take infants, but this young mother has been with me for 14 months. She has been asked to leave every placement she has ever had. The Child Welfare System has no place to put this young mother who will turn 18 in three months. The only thing they could offer was to place the baby in a different home while the mother stayed here until she turned 18 and could access the programs available for single mothers who are adults. I am now being told I cannot be paid for the care of this baby, even though I am the one who is buying the diapers, formula and all the things that go into the care of a low-birth-weight infant. I am also being told that the rate I had been paid for the care of the mother will be cut in half unless I can prove that her behaviors are extreme. The fact that the baby has to be fed every two hours will not be considered. The fact that I gave up one of my emergency placement beds to house this young mother and give her a good start will not be considered. The fact that I lost my retainer on that bed will not be considered. The fact is, I am being asked to care for two children for $520 a month. This is ridiculous. Do you wonder where all your foster parents have gone? Well, get a clue!

I have maintained a teen that every other placement was unable or unwilling to work with. One of these placements cost $3,100 a month. She has been asked to leave every one of them. She has done relatively well here. For my ability to maintain this child when all other placements failed, I am being penalized and my payment for her care is being reduced. What incentive is there for me to take any kid with special needs? I have a skill that has been developed over a period of 30 years of working with children. It has been trained and honed by some of the best trainers available. I have worked in programs where behavior modification techniques were rigidly enforced. I have been taught observation and recording skills, assessment skills and case management. I am good at what I do. I am as much a professional as any social worker or administrator, or legislator in

Washington State. Do not demean the contribution other foster parents, and I have made to the welfare of children in this state. I refuse to accept it. I will be vocal in the defense of foster parenting and the skill required to do it well.

Within the last two years there has been a push to offer legal emancipation to many of the state's dependent children. If teens have a GED and a job, social workers are encouraging them to get emancipated. What 16 or 17-year-old wouldn't be excited by the prospect of being declared a legal adult? The problem is they are not prepared, and they do not realize they are giving up any safety net, like medical and dental care and housing. How many landlords will rent to a 16 1/2-year-old, even if they have a paper stating they are an emancipated minor? They are also giving up monies available for transition through the independent living programs and they are not eligible for the scholarship monies available to kids who turn 18 in the system. Once a judge has signed that order, they are on their own. No help, no net, no going back. Is this really a good outcome? Are there any statistical data being collected on these youth that take the option of legal emancipation before age 18? I don't know of any.

I have been asked by other foster parents to talk about working with young children, and I want to make clear that I am speaking from observation and what other foster parents have shared. In 24 years of foster parenting, I have had three babies in my home because I had pregnant teens that gave birth while in my care. I had a very dear friend and neighbor who did receiving care for young children and I was in her home almost daily.

Children are picked up in all kinds of circumstances and they usually come with only the clothes on their backs. They may be dirty and they may have lice or scabies. They are often ill and malnourished. They may be bruised, battered and burned. They may be drug-affected babies who are going through withdrawal. I remember one child who was brought to my friend's home one evening by the police. He was a five-year-old boy who was so thin every rib showed and his spine protruded down his little back. He was wearing only a pair of dirty short pants and he was wrapped in a blanket the policeman had in his car. I helped her give the child a bath because he was filthy, and I sat with him wrapped in a blanket while she went to find clothing for him to wear. We put pajamas on him and socks on his feet because he was so cold. We offered food, but he only took two bites, and we put him to bed. When we snuggled the covers up around him, he looked at us with large solemn eyes and said, "Thank you for letting me sleep in your bed." This child had been almost starved to death. My friend had to feed him two or three bites of food every hour because his system would not accept more than that. It took about two weeks before he was able to eat normally. She kept him for three months and he was returned to the parent. Over the next five years, this child was removed three more times from his mother's custody and returned to my friend's home. That is hard to witness.

She also had a little 18-month-old girl who had been beaten with a dog chain. I also remember four children who came to her home because the mother had punished the oldest one by holding his hand on a hot stove burner. He had the grid of the hot element burned into his palm.

What does one do with the emotions that come up when you are witness to such horror? One of her little girls had been sodomized and her rectum was so torn that she couldn't control her bowels. She had to have reconstructive surgery.

I have observed that working with younger kids has some of the same requirements, in that a person needs to have a calm demeanor, needs to provide structure and predictability. Children need to be safe, but they also need to feel safe. The feeling of safety comes when kids are able to predict what will happen. That is why routine is so valuable.

When you are working with children who have been abused, it is to be expected that you will see some acting out. They may have night terrors, they may wet the bed, and they may fight going to bed or have trouble staying in bed. They may soil themselves or refuse all efforts at potty train-ing. You may also be asked to deal with children who are autistic or have Asperger's syndrome or other brain-injury issues. Foster parents must learn their own limitations. What are you good at? What are you unwilling to deal with? Many foster parents take only one child at a time. This is prob-ably easier to manage in the larger scheme of things. Some foster parents end up adopting the child they take into their homes. This is a win-win situation, but sometimes the foster parent is led to believe that the child will be legally free to be adopted, and that does not happen.

I know one couple who took a 10-year-old boy who was believed to be unsalvageable. They did so well with him that the social worker asked them to try another really difficult kid. They did well with the second one and ended up with two more. The last child they took was the half-brother of the first child. He has been their greatest challenge because he is a drug baby with ADHD and almost no impulse control. They have managed these boys by running their household like a military school. Everything is controlled, recorded and rewarded by a strict point system. Even evening time hanging out with the adults is earned with good behavior. The kids' rooms are stripped down to almost bare and they earn the use of radio or CD players or books and magazines by good behavior. The foster parents are very careful about what the kids read and what they watch on TV. No comic books, no violent movies, no TV shows with any violent or sexual content. This may seem extreme, but remember, these were "throw-away kids" and their behaviors were extreme. One of the parents is a Unitarian minister and the other one had years of experience working in group homes with very disturbed youth. They are professionals who have put their hearts into turning these kids' lives around. After eight years, it is clear they are succeeding. The oldest child is graduating from high school and preparing to go to college. There is a documentary film being made about this family and they are an inspiration to all of us.

Not all of us can take on those kinds of challenges, but we all bring something special to the table and we, as foster parents, need to be honest with ourselves about what we are and are not willing to do. No foster parent is right for every kid. I decided to work with teens because I really like kids that age. I have worked with young children and was instrumental in getting the Head Start program up and running in Mississippi in 1965. I have worked at Ryther Child Center in the Young Children's Cottage. I have worked with teen boys and with teen girls. I found boys to be more straightforward and girls more complicated, in that they have more social pressures and respond more emotionally to those pressures. These are general statements of what I have observed and not meant to apply to all teen boys or girls. There are certainly many boys who suffer great emotional pain and girls who are able to disregard social pressures.

My decision to work with teen girls was made because I was already working with that population in a group home when I began doing foster care in 1976. It seemed a natural transition to "move my job home." I was dealing with the same kinds of kids, and the things I had learned in that strict behavior modification milieu worked well at my home. "Keep it simple, keep it clear." Hold children accountable, reward good behavior, and communicate expectations clearly. Let kids know what the consequences of bad behavior are. Keep punishments time-limited. Get kids back in good graces quickly. When they are being good, tell them what you see, "I see you turned in all your homework this week. That took a big effort on your part, I'm really proud of you." The kid may shrug it off like it's no big deal, but they will be pleased that you cared enough to notice and they will do it again. The most important thing a foster parent can do is to make a child feel important. They need to know that you care enough to notice the small stuff, to see them as unique and wonderful human beings. You cannot change their past, but you can give them tools to make their future better.

Foster care is supposed to be time limited. Never discount what you can do in a short time. You can change a child's view of the world and of themselves in a short time. Think about your early years growing up and I'll bet you can find a memory of someone who changed your perspective or gave you a new view of yourself. It may have been a teacher or a coach, or a next-door neighbor or the parent of a friend.

The mother of my best friend in third grade influenced me. I had never seen an artist at work and I visited one day when my friend's mother was painting. I had always liked to draw, but art came alive for me that day when I saw that lady putting color on that canvas. To see that painting develop before my eyes was magic. When she turned to me and asked what color I thought the tree should be, I was hooked. I knew at that moment that I was meant to be an artist. I don't know if that lady ever knew she changed my life, but she did. By letting me watch her and engaging me in the process, she gave me a gift beyond price.

Even when there are major issues in the family, that is where resolution needs to happen. If a family can reach out and accept help when they need it, most issues can be worked through. When a child is being subjected to several emotional, physical or sexual abuses, that child needs and deserves to be taken out of the home. The safety of the child must come first. There are times when emotional abuse can be soul killing. I remember one young girl whose mother was very abusing emotionally and she girl felt she was being treated differently than her younger siblings. She couldn't understand why her mother was so abusive. Family counseling was begun and during a session with the whole family present, the mother blurted out that her daughter was the product of a rape and that every time she looked at her, she was reminded of how she was conceived. The girl was devastated. It confirmed her worst fear. She was sure that her mother had a right to hate her and that she was a bad person. I felt the mother had revealed the information to wound her daughter even further. What is a young girl to do with that kind of information? I don't know what happened to this girl because she ran away shortly after that.

Being a foster parent is a very hard job, and we all bring our own baggage and limitations to it. People can learn good parenting skills even when they were not parented well. It is hard to change the pattern, and a person must be willing to do the work to learn new skills. One guideline I use is "Is the child better off emotionally after an interaction with the parent, or do they feel worse about themselves?" A parent can and should enforce rules and expect a level of behavior that is socially expectable. We do not do children any favors by ignoring unacceptable behavior. Even the best kid will mess up sometimes. When that happens, children need to be held accountable. The world will hold them accountable. They need to practice getting past a mistake in judgment in a safe environment. They need to know they can mess up and get past it.

To ground a teenager for three months is not a workable punishment. For a fifteen-year-old, three months seems like a lifetime. They cannot predict their own behavior for that long. Punishment should be predictable, time limited and immediate. When it is over, it's over. One exception

I think might be driving. If a teen is using a car in an irresponsible way, the car should be taken away for a long enough period that the teen learns to respect the responsibility to himself, his parents and society. A teen should not be allowed to carry any passengers in a car until he has driven accident free and ticket free for one year. Teens should also be held responsible for some of the cost of operating the vehicle. It's surprising how much better they drive when they buy their own car. These rules should be talked about several years before a teen reaches the age of getting a driver's license. If you have a conversation about this twice a year for three years before the teen gets a license, the ground rules are already established. They know what to expect if they don't follow the rules. This only works if you are a responsible driver. If you drive like a fool, don't expect your teen not to follow your example. When kids are in foster care, they usually don't get to drive before 18. In order for them to get a license, they must have someone who will be financially responsible and they must be insured, and a foster parent can he held liable for the cost of an accident. I have never accepted that liability, and most foster parents cannot afford to do so. I encourage teens to save some money for driver's education after they turn 18. They can still take the course at most high schools after they have graduated. We have very good public transportation in the Seattle area so teens can get around easily without a car.

Kathleen was 16 and had never been in foster care. She had been living with an aunt, but had been forced to leave when her aunt discovered that Kathleen had been pregnant and had an abortion. Kathleen's mother was a drug user who had abandoned her at an early age and her father was her primary caregiver during her early childhood. Her father had a problem with alcohol and was often abusive to his current domestic partner. Kathleen was clearly upset and did not know what to expect. She expressed how strange it felt to be driven to a stranger's home by a caseworker she didn't know and told that this is where you will live. After we went through the intake interview she seemed to be relieved and did settle in quickly. She got along well with the other kids and she was very bright and articulate. She had a boyfriend who was 18 and had a hot red sports car. He was from a wealthy family. He showered her with expensive gifts. He showed up every morning to transport her to school and was at the school every day to bring her home. After a few months, Kathleen broke off the relationship because she felt he was too controlling and she was not ready for a serious commitment. She became involved with a young man who was severely depressed and had a serious drinking problem. He lost his job and sank deeper in to clinical depression. He also became physically abusive to Kathleen. She left and returned to this relationship three times before she finally escaped it completely. She went into counseling and was able to recognize that she had created the same relationship she had seen with her father and his girlfriends. She was also able to give credit to her father for the strength and wisdom he had given her. She was then able to move on and get more of her own needs met in a more productive relationship.

Each child has his own special needs, and you may find what works well with one will not work with another. You must be an astute observer of human nature and figure out what is important to each child. You will need to go the extra mile many times in working with other people's children.

This next statement is a personal opinion, but I ask you to give it some thought. Don't work with a kid you actively dislike! You can dislike the behavior but still like the kid. Behavior can be changed. If you cannot find something about a child that you like, you owe it to that child to have them placed with someone else. No caregiver can work will all children. Once in a while you will find a child whose energy conflicts with yours so completely that you will find yourself getting hostile just being in the presence of that child. Pay attention to this. It is not a failure on your part or on the child's. It just is. I call it conflicting energetic fields, and it usually can't be worked though or changed or made better. This is when you ask for help. Have the child placed with someone who may be able to work wonders with that child. The child deserves this. Once again I'll stress, I'm not talking about behaviors. Behaviors can be changed. This is deeper and more basic. I have had this happen a few times and I have seen it happen while I worked in group homes. One youth worker would be unable to work with a certain kid when another youth worker would do well with them. Disturbed children have unusually sensitive attention for other people's feelings. They know on a gut level what your true feelings are. You cannot fool them, don't even try. I have worked with, and made connection with, children that many others were unable to reach. I have failed to reach and actually disliked some children that others were quite fond of and worked well with. If you take on the responsibility of working with children, you must be sensitive to your own feelings and realize the child deserves to be with people who can like them on some level, even when they are acting out. You don't have to like the behaviors, but you must like the child.

Not all situations are fixable. Latoya was a 16-year-old, mixed-race child. She was chubby and light-skinned with curly hair. She had a beautiful smile and a pleasant demeanor. She had been raised on the streets and she had been running drugs for her older brother since she was six years old. She said no one ever expected a six-year-old on the playground to be a dealer, but her brother would tell her who to approach and she would make the exchange and bring the money back to her brother. Her mother was an addict and all her siblings were drug-affected at birth also. They were in the business of selling drugs. That is how they lived. Latoya could not read and could write very few words. She was actually very bright, but so learning-disabled she was non-functional in a school setting. For two years Latoya bounced in and out of my home. She and I made some connection on a spirit level and we both knew that she would stay just long enough to get cleaned up and rest a few days before she would run away and go back to the streets.

Latoya always respected my house rules. She never stole from me and she could be sweet and funny. Once in awhile she would let her guard down and let me see the sadness in her life. I never judged her or criticized her because I knew she was dealing with life the only way she knew. She aged out of the system three years ago and I have not seen her since. I heard that she was living in Tacoma with her brother's girlfriend while her brother was in jail. I was the only home in King County that would take Latoya because her history was so bad. I don't know why I was willing to take that chance, but I'm glad I did. I felt a great compassion for her and sadness that there was nothing I could do to make her life better in any meaningful way. I asked her once what she expected to do when she grew up. Her answer was, "I'll be dead at an early age or in prison." I hope that's not what happens, but I think she was being realistic about her future.

Ninety percent of children born with fetal alcohol or fetal drug effect will be involved in the court system. We have one of the highest incidences of fetal alcohol or fetal drug effect in the nation. These children are born with a burden they must carry all their life. I don't know why King County and the greater Seattle area has such a high incidence of these disorders, but a great many of these children will end up in foster care and we, as foster parents, will be witness to their struggles and their pain.

In an earlier chapter I had shared ambivalence about renewing my license. I did renew it because I could not bring myself to back out on the two teens in my home who were both 17 years old and needed care for a few more months. I found this re-licensing process to be the worst I have experienced in 24 years of doing foster care. The licensor demanded access to my health care records and I had to sign a release form for my doctor to discuss my mental, physical, and emotional health. The fact that I had 24 years with the department and a record of providing excellent care meant nothing. I had to provide financial records proving that I have sufficient income to provide for my household. I had to provide building records and inspection records for my home. The licensor questioned why I had so many smoke detectors. I have one in every room, but I am only required to have two. She asked if I planed to get married or if I dated. She told Lisa that if she dated, she had to provide a babysitter that was approved by the state. Lisa has no small children, her son is 15 years old, and one of us is always in the home at all times. She also required that my grandson have a criminal history check done when he turns 16 and that any family member who visits here should also have one done. She read each WAC code and discussed whether or not it applied to me. WAC says you must have a potty-chair, you don't need one, etc. All these things may be necessary, but the effect is to treat foster parents like offenders.

During the last two years a great many foster parents have quit. The complete lack of understanding of what we are being asked to do is one reason. The reduction in compensation and lack of respect is another reason.

The people most affected by all this are the kids. Two weeks ago I was asked to return from my vacation time and accept a 14-year-old girl because there was no bed available in King County or Snohomish County. Once again, kids are being kept in DSHS offices over the weekend because there are no placements available. Social workers are being asked to do more and more. Foster parents are being required to transport kids to supervised visits, and to supervise the visit, but are being told they should not talk to the parents they are supervising because they are not trained in supervision. People are being hired as foster parent retention specialists to stem the tide of people who are saying enough is enough!

I received a flyer about a foster parent meeting last month and I attended it. The plan is to try and create support cells in geographic areas so we will have other foster parents to share ideas with and to support each other. This is a great idea, but it's somewhat like reinventing the wheel. We had this for many years and it does work.

Create community, give respect to your providers, and they will tell you what they need and want. Pay them enough to compensate for their time and expenses in working with children who require constant supervision. It's a lot cheaper than locking up these children. We cannot take on the responsibility of other people's children and then leave them unsupervised while working a 50-60 hour week. This is completely unrealistic. When kids enter the foster care system, they come with many varied special needs. Their most immediate need is safety and security. They need an adult in charge who will be willing to work with them to overcome the problems in their life. That means being there 24 hours a day.

I do not wish to discourage anyone from becoming a foster parent. It is an opportunity to enrich your own life while helping a child in need. Give what you can and enjoy the ride, but do so with your eyes wide open. Know that this is hard work. It is more difficult than parenting your own children. You will encounter a multiplicity of problems. You will work with some awesome people and some jerks. You will get frustrated with some of the things you are asked to do and you must learn to set good boundaries. You will grow and you will have the satisfaction of knowing that you have made a difference in someone's life. When you see a child grow and succeed in life, you know that you had a part in it, you know it's a worthwhile way to spend your life.

I have written this book for two purposes. I want the general population to know that kids in foster care are not bad people. They need understanding, love and acceptance. My second purpose is to encourage others to become foster parents. I have loved sharing my home and my heart with these children. My hope is that a few administrators will also read this and get a different view about what we as foster parents really do. I know hard choices must sometimes be made about budget cuts and what services can and should be provided, but when you cut the rates of foster parents who are taking your most difficult kids, you are being short-sighted. When you cut people trained as supervisors and expect foster parents to take on that role for free, you are being negligent. When children are spending weekends in offices because you have no available beds or are being sent to the other side of the state for placement, some things need to change.

I started doing foster care because I could stay home and care for my own children and manage a health problem at the same time. I have done foster care for 24 years. Under your current guidelines, I would not be given a license. Many single parents would become foster parents if it would benefit them by allowing them to care for other people's children while they cared for their own. You pay people to do elder care so those seniors can remain in their home. Why not do the same for children? If I am willing to stay home and take care of the state's dependent children, I should be compensated. It is a real job! It is a profession, and I refuse to let some children's services administrators define it as a volunteer position. That demeans us, our skill level and the importance of what we do. We, as foster parents take on the most important task of helping children who have special needs, who are in crisis, who are victims of abuse. We love them, nurture them and release them when the time comes. We open our homes, our hearts and our families to these children.

I was called at 12:45 AM last night about taking an 11-year-old girl. The social worker was desperate because there was no placement available for this child. I refused to take her. I refused because she was younger than the scope of my license. If there were a problem, I would have been held responsible. The lack of support for foster homes forces us to make these kinds of hard choices. I fear that this child spent the night in the social worker's office. I know this is happening more and more frequently, even though it is in direct conflict with the state's own placement guides.

The Children's Administration put out a memo in November 2004, which includes this paragraph: "At the Children's Administration, we remain committed to improving outcomes for children and families within the public child welfare system. This memo reaffirms our expectations and our commitment to placement practices that result in good outcomes for children. We will continue our efforts to strengthen practices in the field and support the important work that social workers and foster parents are providing to children and families." If this is truly the aim of this administration, why have so may foster parents quit the system? Why are children sleeping in offices? Why are children being kept out of schools because the short-term emergency placements are so short-term that kids can't go to school? Where have all the families gone who once were the backbone of the foster care system? How much money have we really saved and how many children are paying the price for the cost-cutting measures the state is using that have all but destroyed the foster care system in Washington State? We can do better!

When the directive came down from the top two years ago to cut every possible thing from the foster care system, the result made it nearly impossible for foster parents to be paid anything above basic foster care rates. So the system lost some of its best people. Lost were the people with the skills and training to care for the special needs kids, the kids with FAS and FAE and the kids with behavior problems that require extra skilled caregivers. The Children's Administration wrote these children off, and is failing to provide the level of care sufficient to produce a good outcome. They failing at their own guidelines. How well is that working for the administrators, for the children and for the future of the children in Washington State?

Isn't it time to take a hard look at current policies and get back to a more common sense approach to foster care? People who do foster care deserve to be compensated at a level that makes it feasible for them to do it. People who work with special needs kids need to be compensated for their skill level and the extra time to manage these behaviors.

I am still here, but a lot of good people aren't. Again, how well is that working? Children Services administrators may be able to balance their books, but from the perspective of a caregiver, the policies are completely failing to meet established guidelines.

Let's all get back to what we have in common, genuine belief that we must help children who cannot help themselves. Supportive parenting can help all children. The state needs foster parents who are skilled, trained, and dedicated to the protection and nurture of children.

Either pay foster parents or develop a system of state-supported group homes. These could be assessment centers that take kids for a month or two while the case is being worked to determine the best outcome for the child. If a child then needed long-term foster care, he would be moved into that system if a good match was found and the outcome for the child would be better. This is an expensive option, but it works well in other states that have tried it.

Another option is to go back to the receiving home model where a child can stay up to 90 days. Pay foster parents a decent retainer to be on call 24 hours a day. Realize that people doing receiving care cannot work outside their homes and that the issues of short-term care are different from long-term care. Realize that caring for teens is a lot more expensive than caring for babies and young children. The issues are different. Support your teen parents so that they have a chance to get basic skills and become effective parents.

The last option I want to mention is to look at what is being done in other countries. In England, France, Australia, and Canada, foster parents are state workers. They are given a house, paid a salary and have the same status as teachers. I know Washington State is not that progressive yet, but it is worth putting on the table.

The fact remains, our system is currently broken and it needs to be fixed. There should be places available when a child needs placement. Foster parenting is worthwhile and rewarding. I am glad I have spent the last thirty years working with children. I would do it all over again, even though the system is imperfect. It has been a great adventure.

After another unpleasant interaction with the Department of Licensed Resources, I had to rethink what I was doing.

A licenser that I had issues with in the past filed a complaint because she had come to my house unannounced and found two of my foster kids alone. One was 15 and one was 17 years old. I had taken another child to the orthodontist and the girls had plans to take the bus and visit friends.

Their bus came 20 minutes after I left and they were waiting in the house. She (the licenser) contended that no foster child could be left alone and I was negligent because I had left them inside the house. She felt that I should have put them out and made them wait at the bus stop.

When I found out that the licenser who filed the complaint was going to be the investigator, I filed a counter complaint saying my civil rights were being violated. The Department of Child Welfare agreed with me and a ruling was made that a person filing a complaint could not investigate the complaint.

Her complaint was dismissed as unfounded and the rule clarified that a child under 12 could not be left alone. Sometimes I wonder what ever happened to common sense.

Dear Rita,

I don't think I could ever express in words my gratitude to you. You have shown me what it means to be caring and truly understanding. I am grateful for people like you who strive to make people's lives better, although there is really no reward to be gained other than as I mentioned, gratitude.

Thank you for being so humble in offering your home and your help to me, for these things I will always be grateful. You have been more than anyone could ask in terms of help.

My mother and I have not had the relationship. I wish we did, but having you there has made this transition a lot easier for me. You are one of the most admirable people I have had the chance of meeting. You are more than a foster mother, grandmother, and mother; you are a creative, compassionate, brilliant woman, the kind whose spirit can never grow old. I thank God for making the opportunity of meeting a real one.

I am not thankful for my life situation. I believe everything happens for a purpose and hopefully will grow stronger from this experience.

Thank you for everything, Love Always, Monica

AT THAT POINT, I DECIDED NOT TO ACCEPT ANY NEW placements for a while and I went to work at Ryther Child Center in their Adolescent Drug Treatment Program. It was a great growth opportunity for me because I had to examine and give up a lot of feelings and opinions I had about people with substance abuse issues.

Many of the staff at the Boy's Cottage where I worked were in recovery. I found them to be very knowledgeable and professional. I came to greatly admire their dedication to helping the boys in the program learn the skills to begin their own recovery.

The program had a level system and the boys progressed through the levels as they accepted responsibility for their own behavior. Most of the kids were in their mid-teens, but some were as young as 12 and a few had turned 18, but were still in high school. Very few came to the program willingly. Most were court ordered because of criminal activity and faced jail time if they didn't complete treatment. They came with the attitude that they could "work the system," but the program was designed to confront that belief quickly.

The first 3 days the boys were on lock down and could not go out of the cottage at all. They were going through withdrawal and were most likely to run from the program at that time.

The day began at 7:00 AM and the boys had 30 minutes to get dressed and ready for breakfast. They had to be wearing "day wear," no PJs, and no house shoes. Breakfast was served at 7:30. Everyone had to stand behind his chair while the rules were read and each kid had to say three things they were grateful for. There were strict rules about conversations, and they were not allowed to talk about drugs or about street life and violence of any kind. They could not use putdowns or any sexual innuendos.

The staff ate with the kids and monitored behavior and conversations. Points were given or taken away depending on their behavior. No sugar or caffeine was allowed.

After breakfast was chore time and each kid was assigned a chore for a week. They got points for how well they did their chore and they had opportunity to earn extra points by doing extra work. After chores were completed and checked off, they had shower time and were required to shave and brush their teeth and get ready for the morning group. They each had a workbook and it was checked at group to see if they had completed their assignments. Many of these boys could not read well and their writing ability was very limited. This proved to me once again that early school achievement is vital for young people to succeed and no child should get to 6th grade unable to read and write.

Morning group was about drug education, taught by a chemical dependency counselor. Kids talked about their usage and behavior and were confronted about their drug thinking. This included examining attitudes and behavior and how that affected their lives. Many of the clients had grown up in homes where one or both parents were using. One of the things I found shocking was that many of the kids were introduced to drugs by their parents.

The scores from the previous day were read and behaviors discussed in the group and kids gave feedback to each other about what they were seeing. Sometimes they were brutal with each other, but generally they tried to be supportive, while being honest about what they were seeing. A lot of kids had started using drugs at an early age and had not developed very good social skills. This created interesting group dynamics as they jockeyed for position. Some kids told tall tales to impress and others tried to hide emotionally.

Their workbooks were checked and they were given follow-up assignments. They had to write about why they used drugs, how they felt when they did, reasons for stopping and how they felt about getting clean and staying clean. This was all designed to break through the denial that all addicts use and to get in touch with honest feelings that they were covering up with drugs.

Many of the kids were depressed and physically very deconditioned. Many were malnourished and had bad teeth or serious skin infections. Kids who had been using meth were usually in very poor condition. They had open sores on their body and various rashes and scarring where the meth was being worked out of their system.

After group, there was always some kind of physical activity. It was basketball or running or tag football. One of the staff members would take a group of kids to run up and down stairs that can be found outside all over Seattle because the streets are so hilly. I think he knew every outside staircase in the county.

Kids entering the program were so out of shape, this was very hard for them, but within a week you could see their fitness building as they responded to healthy living and exercise. It was also a way for the teens to get in touch with their body in a positive way.

Afternoons were taken up with more groups and individual counseling with social workers and primary counselors. Twice a week they had family meetings and visiting hours, but the list of who could visit was very limited.

When teens reached a certain level, they were taken to AA or NA meetings in the community. This was to help establish the habit of outside support and the teens looked forward to the meetings. There were girls there and people with cigarettes and coffee, none of which they were supposed to use. But once again, they had to learn to deal with temptation and the real world, and they had to have a clean Urine Analysis after the meeting to retain their ability to go off the locked unit.

The most likely infraction was cigarettes. Almost all the teens smoked, and the nicotine habit seemed harder to break than illegal drugs. If they had a dirty UA, they also had their level dropped and had to repeat that phase of treatment.

Like all milieus, there were staff members who were hardnosed, by the book, and tried to catch everything, and there were staff members who were more lenient in how they interpreted the rules. This set up conflicts among the staff because each group felt it was right. The staff ranged in age from young people just out of college to people in their 50s. I was the oldest staff member and that gave me a real advantage in working with the boys. I could be very nurturing and very strict at the same time. Word passed quickly among the boys; don't mess with Grandma Rita.

One of my favorite things was being the art teacher. I taught the boys how to draw landscapes, portraits and rocks. I brought in a large pastel board and each boy drew a rock to represent the hard things they were trying to overcome. We then drew water and sand and a large fish swimming upstream. That was to show that even when you have problems, other things are going on around you that are positive. It was a beautiful piece of art work and the boys were proud of their part in creating it.

Most of the kids were convinced they could not draw, but I made it so simple they were unafraid to try. I also brought in art that was nontraditional so they could see examples. They were amazed to see the work of Marc Chagall with people floating in the air and chickens larger than people. It was freeing to know he was so famous and that he followed none of the rules of perspective.

During these lessons, the boys became kids having fun, and that was one of the biggest goals. Most young addicts don't know how to have fun without being stoned. They never learned the simple pleasure of a walk in the woods or a hard game of basketball or creating something. Drugs were their recreation and motivation. The business of buying, selling and using, and getting money to continue takes over their whole life. That's what addiction is all about.

Most teens are searching for their true identity, and when you add drugs to the process, growth stops.

One of the staff members at the treatment center had a prior history of using drugs from the age of 12 until he was 35, when he finally got clean and sober. He then began learning the skills needed to handle his life as an adult. While he was using drugs, he never had a driver's license or rented an apartment. He had no credit history, had never held a steady job, and lived off the grid. When he worked, he was paid cash, under the table so he earned no social security credits. He had been to jail many times for petty theft, but luckily never got caught for a major crime and had never gone to prison. He went to treatment three times before he was able to get clean and stay clean.

When I heard his story, I was amazed because I could not see him in that light. To me, he was a competent man who was very good at his job. I found myself surprised at the history of many of the people I worked with. It proved to me that people can change and go on to lead productive lives even after years of addiction.

While I was at Ryther, two staff members relapsed and were fired. I came to understand that addiction is a lifetime challenge and an addict is always an addict no matter how long they have been clean. If the right circumstance occurs, they may be at risk of relapse.

There were people from all ethnic backgrounds and socio-economic levels. Some ethnic groups are at higher risk for alcoholism because they don't have the enzyme to convert alcohol to sugar and become addicted very quickly. Native Americans are at very high risk; Hispanics often have the same risk level.

The boys were given journals to write in daily. One of my duties was to focus on their feelings and to be honest about their emotions. It was also a way for them to share feelings privately with someone who could give them positive feedback or point out thought patterns that were not working for them. One of the first things the boys did each morning was go to the journal box and read the response to what they had written the day before. I could see progress in their journals as they progressed through the program.

Having twelve teen boys in a group can be a set-up for problems, so behavior was highly controlled. The residents were not allowed to touch each other, even playfully. Any staff member could call a "clear the floor" command, and all the boys had to go at once into their room. Anyone who did not was not allowed to stay in the program. Any damage done to the cottage was charged to the client. The boys were earning money by doing their chores, by compliance and by bidding on extra chores. They did not like to lose money, so they tended to be cautious about damage.

When a youth was near completion, he could call a "Grad" meeting and request feedback about what he needed to complete the program. All staff members had to be in agreement that he was ready. Then a date was set and family and friends were invited to share in the celebration. Cake and soft drinks were provided, and we would all speak about what we had seen as the graduate progressed through the program and what strengths he had gained. He was presented with his graduation certificate, any awards he had earned, and a check for the money in his account. It was very emotional and moving to see these young boys make such great changes in a few weeks and to know they now had a chance to own their lives again.

The boys often called back after leaving the program to touch base and let us know how they were doing. We could accept their calls, but could have no other contact for two years after the client left the program.

The rules of confidentiality were very strict, and staff members were good at keeping these rules. Every piece of paper had to be accounted for and we could not even mention a client's name or say if they were in the program if someone called for them.

Once again, I witnessed how good people were, willing to work at low paying, hard, intense jobs to help young people change their future and give them a chance for a better life. I was glad to be a part of that.

My family knew I enjoyed my job at Ryther, but they were encouraging me to quit because the shift work was hard on me. At about the same time, I was approached by a favorite social worker about a "special needs" 16-year-old who needed placement. She had been diagnosed as schizophrenic, was on meds and compensating well. I decided to give it a try, and I went to part time status at Ryther and took the teen into my home.

She was a tall attractive young woman who was being raised by an alcoholic father. Her mother was mentally ill and unable to care for her.

She applied for a job at a local McDonalds and was hired. Her self-esteem improved greatly. She continued in her school program and was doing well, but she tried to become her father's caretaker as his health failed. She would give him her check and often stole food from my cupboards to take to her dad. He finally decided to go into treatment, and she was overjoyed at the prospect of her dad finally getting control of his alcoholism. He completed treatment and she was hopeful that she could soon return to her father's care.

When her father relapsed, it was a crushing blow to her. She began refusing to take her meds and her behavior became more unstable. She quit her job at McDonalds and asked to be moved into an independent living program. She was now 17 and 5 months old and the social worker felt that was a good idea, so she could have continued care until she was 21. She left my home after being with us almost two years. I heard that her father died and she had been hospitalized, but stabilized, and had graduated from high school and entered college. Mental illness is such a challenge, but one thing I have observed is that people who suffer from these problems can lead productive lives if they have support.

I continued to work at Ryther on a part-time basis, which was often 30 hours a week or more. I was scheduled for a night shift when the weather turned bad. November in the Seattle area is known for very unstable weather and we sometimes have major storms. I left for work at 9:00 PM because I knew the conditions were such that I probably couldn't get there if I waited until 11:00.

I got to the cottage at 9:30 and the boys were agitated. The wind was blowing so hard that the trees were losing limbs and debris was flying in the air. The evening AA meeting was cancelled because the conditions were so adverse.

At bedtime, the boys were reluctant to go to bed and then the power went out. Suddenly these teen boys were frightened ten-year-olds. We had emergency lighting that kept the hallways and bathrooms lit, but there were no lights in the boys' rooms or the common rooms. Several boys asked if they could sleep in the living room and we agreed to allow this. They asked to turn on the TV and the stereo, and had to be reminded that those things required power to operate.

I decided to read a book to the boys and, using a flashlight, I began to read. This seemed to calm them and slowly they each decided to make their way back to their beds where they could be warm under their covers.

By that time, the cottage was pretty cold because the heat also required electricity. I didn't mention to the boys that we only had 4 hours of backup power, to about 1:00 AM, and we scrambled to find every available battery for the flashlights. We placed one 12 volt flashlight on each floor aimed at the ceiling, and this provided enough light to find the bathrooms.

We took bets as to whether the batteries would last or daylight would come first. The security system also required electricity and the door locks would not operate, so as the weather got wilder, the doors were being sucked open by the wind. We were doing 15-minute bed checks and hoping that the large old trees would survive the storm and not come crashing down on the building.

Daylight revealed the extent of the damage and, as I made my way home, I had to detour around fallen trees and all kinds of things that littered the roadways. I live in unincorporated King County and our area took a huge hit from the storm. It looked like a war zone. We had two downed trees from our yard, but the neighbors were hard at work clearing the streets of fallen timber.

The electricity stayed out for a week at my home and we cooked and stayed warm with the two fireplaces. The electricity was back on at Ryther in two days. I looked forward to going to work just to get warm.

My son, Mark, and his wife came to visit and to spend Thanksgiving with us. We had a lovely visit. We talked a lot about the film Mark was finishing and how good he felt about it. I noticed that Mark had a fine tremor in his hands and questioned him about it. He said he thought he had a pinched nerve in his neck that was causing it. He planned to check it out as soon as he finished the post production on the film.

About two weeks later, I got a call from my daughter-in-law, Celia, telling me Mark was in the hospital in Intensive Care because he had passed out at his drumming circle and had a seizure. He was rushed to the ER and they found a brain tumor. I was able to catch the next available flight to Burbank because I only had two girls at home and in school, and my grown daughter was able to care for them while I was gone. My daughter-in-law picked me up at the airport and we drove to the hospital.

Mark had been transferred to University Hospital Neurosurgery Intensive Care. I was numb with fear. We got to the hospital and were required to go through metal detectors to enter. Then we had to stand in line to get an arm band that designated where we were going, what floor we could get off on and who we were visiting. There was an armed guard at the elevator and we had to show our arm band before being allowed to enter.

We proceeded to the Neurosurgical Wing and entered a waiting room. It was filled with people, and there was a sign directing us to use a phone at the end of the hall to request entry to the ICU Unit. There were two police officers at the door. We finally made it inside. There was a large nurse's station in the center of the room with all the patients placed like spokes on a wheel. Everything was open, but there were privacy curtains that could be drawn around each bed.

Mark was lying with his head elevated, and his face lit up when he saw me. He was awake and lucid, and it was hard to imagine that he was gravely ill. In "Mark fashion," he had already made friends; he introduced me to his bed mates and to his nurse. Mark, having always been charismatic, was interested in knowing everyone he came in contact with. People responded to that energy in a very positive way. It was hard to equate this strong handsome man with these surroundings.

The surgeons came in and showed us the x-rays that showed a walnut-sized tumor at the base of the spine where it entered the skull. He explained that it was blocking the spinal fluid, and they planned to put in shunts to reroute the spinal fluid around the tumor. They said that the tumor could not be removed because of its location. Trying to remove the tumor would cause major trauma to the brain, but there were other options, and the shunts would buy time to get other treatments in place. I know these words were meant to give hope and comfort, but when I looked at my son, I knew this would not end well. He was a candle burning brightly, and I knew that light, which touched so many people, would soon leave us.

When we left the ICU, I broke down and cried. My daughter-in-law could not comfort me. She just couldn't go there yet. An Indian man, whose wife was in the ICU recovering from a major stroke, held my hand and let me cry. He offered what comfort he could and encouraged me to be strong. We met many times in that crowded waiting room after that and somehow drew some strength from each other.

He told me he and his wife had retired and moved to L.A. to live with his son and daughter-in-law, and they took care of the grandchildren while the parents both worked. His wife never learned to speak English, he said, though she was only 40 when they left India. He told me his son worked for Hershey Corp. and how proud he was of his children. Every day I would ask about his wife and he would tell me she was still critical, and I would talk about Mark and his family. I never learned this man's name and I never told him mine, but it didn't matter. His face would light up when he saw me and he would reach for my hand. We were both sitting vigil and knowing we could do nothing but wait. I look back at that time and wish I could say "Thank you" because that human contact was a gift beyond price.

After the surgery to install the stents, Mark had some aphasia and it was difficult for him to communicate. At that point, the doctors put him on meds to control the swelling in his brain, and he was able to go home.

He was losing strength and weight very rapidly, yet he still wanted to participate in the things he loved to do. He went to Drumming Circle in a wheelchair and to a dance performance and a concert by the band, "Blind Boys of Alabama." His spirit kept reaching out to life.

There were more trips to the hospital and more procedures, and his wife and daughters cared for him with tenderness and love as he grew weaker. Friends and family members came to visit, and Mark was lucid and able to enjoy their company. He was not in a great deal of pain, but within a month he could not get out of a chair without help. He had a lot of nausea and almost constant hiccoughs.

Celia, his wife, and Maia and Riva, his daughters, were trying to work and maintain some income for the family, and we were all trying to provide the care Mark needed. The love in that family was a beautiful thing to see, and I know my son was blessed to have a wife and daughters who cared for him with all their hearts.

A neighborhood church in Pasadena, where Mark and his family were members, organized a rotating dinner delivery and every day a church member brought dinner to the house. This was a great help and so appreciated.

I would sit with Mark when Celia worked, and while we listened to music, I would rub his feet and exercise his hands. We didn't talk a lot, but the silence was comfortable. In the evenings, Celia would read aloud to Mark and he looked forward to that every day.

Mark's brother, sister and nephew came to visit, and Jason would take Mark outside into the garden and sit in the sun with him. Mark's friend, Dennis, came from Seattle and spent time with Mark. We were all saying our goodbyes while praying for a miracle to save him.

It was not to be, and three-and-a-half months after diagnosis, Mark passed away peacefully at home with his family around him. He was such a remarkable man and touched so many lives in a positive way.

After Mark passed away, his wife and two daughters took his largest drum to the park where his drumming circle met, where they left it with several bottles of wine and cups, along with his picture and a note saying

"Rest in Peace Mark." It was what Mark would have wanted: "Celebrate my life and have a glass of wine on me!"

The drumming circle at the park included Vietnam Vets, homeless people, young Hispanic men, Native Americans, and many local musicians who just wanted to feel the vibe of the drums.

How do you go on after that kind of loss? The only way I could deal with it was to stay busy, so I went back to operating the foster home and I volunteered at Ryther. I taught art in the Boys' Cottage.

I also had to define my own faith, and I knew Mark was in a better place and free from that body that no longer worked. I know he is a living spirit and I am grateful that I was chosen to be the mother of such a wonderful person. I still miss him every day.

Mom-

Mom you are the greatest! You took me in your house and took care of me. You gave me advice and comforted me when I was down. You told me to put my head up and be proud. Whenever I had something on my mind, you were there to talk to. When I needed help you were always there to coach me. When I was doing things wrong you told me what was right. You made me feel wanted and warm when I was unwanted and cold. So now I say thank you for being there through all the hard times, because you made my face shine with happiness.

Love, Liz

THE FOSTER CARE SYSTEM CONTINUES TO TRY TO REINVENT ITSELF and is failing. It is less functional now than it was 30 years ago. Though there are more checks and balances in place, there will always be good homes and homes where children are not well cared for. The only way to change that will be to make foster parents state employees and give them the same status as teachers with the same oversights. That is done in other countries, but it is an expensive option and not likely to happen here.

The teens in my home are getting fewer services now than they were receiving 30 years ago. As the money dries up, the least able are the ones who are hit the hardest. More and more medical and dental offices are refusing to take "Provider One," the medical coverage for foster kids, so it is harder to get services for the kids in the area where I live. I drive to Seattle for dental care for the kids and use a clinic in Kenmore for medical because most providers in Kirkland will not take Provider One.

Last year two sisters were placed with me. These children were the most challenging I have ever had. They were abandoned at an early age by their birth mother and they bounced around between relatives and the foster care system for most of their lives. Both girls were learning disabled and one had Fetal Alcohol Syndrome. They fought with each other and with the other teens in the home. The older girl, who was 17 years old, was highly sexualized and I suspected she was prostituting. The younger one had no impulse control and would regularly sneak out the window after curfew.

I knew I was not able to provide the security these girls needed and I asked to have them placed in a more secure setting. It took several weeks for a placement to be found and, during that time, I knew that if anything happened to them I would be held responsible.

That can be pretty frightening. We, as foster parents, are sometimes asked to do more than is possible in a home setting, and we cannot fix every child. We must advocate for ourselves as we advocate for children. We should not assume responsibility for the fact that the system is failing to provide resources for those most disturbed, hard to place children. These are the kind of children who benefit from a structured group home setting with around-the-clock staffing and a good behavior modification program in place. Unfortunately, most of these resources are closed now because they are expensive to operate.

I have been asked by several people to write about what works in parenting teens. When I think about what works, I keep coming back to my list I call "The Abilities." In order to teach them, you have to live them.

1. PREDICTABILITY.

Children should be able to count on a parent or caregiver to be predictable. That requires being consistent with rules, expectations and reactions. It means making sure your message doesn't change with your mood. If a child is expected to make their bed every day and change their sheets on Saturday, there should be a consistent consequence for not doing it. Start young and build habits that will last a lifetime. An unmade bed might mean a 30 minute earlier bedtime on the day the bed was unmade. If you choose to make this an issue, you must be willing to make your own bed every day. If an unmade bed is not important to you, choose another issue. Just make sure to be consistent so the child can predict the action and the consequence.

2. ACCOUNTABILITY.

Life holds us all accountable. Children should be able to count on you to do what you say you will. If you are expected to show up for work and you don't, you may lose your job. If a child has homework and doesn't do it, they may fail their class.

If a parent is not accountable to their partner, there will be no trust in the relationship and it could destroy the family system. Accountability means you can be trusted.

There will be times when a child will break that trust. Hopefully it will be a small breach and it can become a teachable moment. Children don't like to lose your trust, but sometimes they don't think things through. That's when it's important to let them know you are disappointed they made that decision.

Keep the focus on the action; i.e., "I am really disappointed that you made the decision to skip school today. That's going to make me question your judgment in the future and I will have to keep a closer eye on you to make sure you are using good judgment. Your consequence is..." (whatever you as a parent decide), but keep it short, direct and time limited. Being grounded for a month is excessive and only fosters resentment. It teaches nothing. For a 15-year-old, a month seems like forever.

Don't say something like, "You are really stupid and I'll never trust you because you lied about going to school." Attack the action, not the person. Don't be afraid to let them know you will be checking on their attendance and that you will hold them accountable even if they don't like it.

3. RELIABILITY.

I rely upon my brakes to stop my car. If I need them and they don't work, I could have a serious accident. It's another word meaning you trust.

Can your child rely on you to provide the basic needs of food, shelter and safety? Can your child trust you to try to understand even when they mess up? Can your child rely on you to love them just the way they are and to help them grow up with the skills needed to lead a productive life? Can they rely on you not to use physical or emotional violence in your parenting?

You see by now that my list has everything to do with the parents' ability to handle their own lives and, in so doing, to provide a road map for the child to grow into a successful adult. The hardest thing about parenting is being responsible for your own behavior. Your behavior becomes the expectation for the child.

The needs of a 13-year-old are very different from those of a six-year-old or a 17-year-old. Each age has a function to teach the child the necessary skills to grow up. At six, a child is learning to build social relationships and to navigate the school environment, but they are totally dependent on the adults in their life to provide food, shelter, safety, and emotional support.

There are so many single parent households that even these can stretch a parent thin and it's very hard to do more than survive. A parent comes home from work tired and needs to prepare food, monitor homework, and do household chores, shopping, and all the other duties of managing a family.

Engage your child in the process. Give your child chores they can do in a short time. These might be to set the table, gather up dirty laundry and place it by the washing machine, pick up toys or magazines from the living room. A six-year-old can do any of these. Don't forget to say thank you to your child.

Sit down to a meal and eat with your child. Eat at the table and turn off the TV and cell phones during the meal. The bonding that happens when people eat together is well known. It is also a time to talk with your child and find out if there are any problems that you need to be aware of. Keep your ears open to what your child is saying. Ask questions children can answer (What did you do for recess today? Who is your best friend? What do you like about them?).

You may hear things you aren't expecting, like "He keeps the other boys from beating me up." Keep your voice at a normal level and ask more questions until you have a true picture of what your child is telling you. You may really never know if you don't have "face time" with your child. Limit TV time and pay attention to homework time.

Many children have trouble learning to read or to do basic math. If you don't find this out by second grade, your child will suffer throughout his school years and may drop out. Do not assume that your child will catch up or that the teacher will take care of it. Many bright, gifted children do not learn well with the conventional methods used today. Phonetic reading does not work for some kids. If your child isn't reading, insist on testing. Whatever the test results show, the responsibility falls on the parent to teach what the school can't. The window of time is short; don't delay!

One of the methods I have found successful is memorization with clues. Make this time limited! Tell your child, "We are only going to work on this for 20 minutes each night!

Make flash cards with index cards. Use a marker and print one word on each card. Begin with opposites, like "Up, Down, Me, You, Run, Walk, Go, Stop, Gold, Silver, White, Black." Take 10 cards and read them out loud to your child. Then say, "This is not up, it is..." Let the child guess the opposite. When he guesses right, then have him say it, spell it (out loud) and write it. When he has done 10 words, stop and tell him he has learned 10 new words today, and put them in a pile and mark them, "Words I Know." The next day, do a quick review and see how many he remembers. If it is only two, that's progress and give clues for any he can't remember.

You are building dendrites in the brain. Remember, See it! Say it! Spell it! Write it! Your child could learn 300 words a month this way and he will begin to see patterns and sounds. The important thing is to keep it short, keep it simple, make it fun and help him to see he can learn. This really works!

This works with basic math, adding, subtracting and multiplying. Keep it short. Keep it simple. Stay with numbers under 10. Don't make this hard. It is already hard for the child who can't read. You want to make it easy. In six months, you will have a reader who knows he can learn. This can change your child's life because a child who can't read will see himself as stupid, even if he has a very high IQ.

You will benefit because you will not have to monitor homework for 12 years. You are giving your child the gift of knowing he can learn. It is worth the effort!

When children become teens, their world changes, and parenting a teen can be challenging. It can also be fun and rewarding because you will begin to see the persons they will become.

Remember what your child was like at three years old. You will see these behaviors multiplied a hundred times at 13. If a child was shy and fearful at three years old, they will often be uncomfortable with calling attention to themselves at 13. They may prefer activities that are not competitive. This is not a fixed trait, but a tendency and there is a place for every child to excel. Helping them to find things they are good at will help them gain self-esteem. Remember self-esteem comes after achievement, not before. You cannot praise a child into feeling good about themselves.

Do not withhold praise when they do well. They need to be recognized for achievement. Always comment on a job well done, even if it's scrubbing the bathtub!

All 13-year-olds I've ever worked with feel they don't fit in, and they are afraid of being rejected by their peers. That's why they are so vulnerable. They want to fit in and be accepted, and this can change on a daily basis. The social scene in middle school is one of the most stressful things your child will ever face. That's is why it's vital that they feel loved and supported at home. Seventh, eighth and ninth grades are when your child is most likely to be exposed to drugs, alcohol and sex. Don't think it won't happen to your kid. It will. You have to be the safe harbor so they can talk about the pressures.

At 13, every boy is dealing with a body that is changing so rapidly he doesn't know from day to day what to expect or how it will function. There is the whole issue of hormones and body odor, and hair and peer pressure. You as a parent will suddenly become uncool. They cannot believe you were ever 13, or that you could ever understand what they are going through and what they are feeling.

In fact, the world is changing so rapidly that parents did grow up in a different world. This is a time to be hyper-vigilant and somewhat invisible at the same time. If you have liquor in the house, lock it up. If you have firearms, get a gun safe.

Before you say, "My kid would never," I would remind you that your job is to protect, and you don't know what pressures your young teen may be facing. You don't know what your child's friends may do. I've had teens tell me about adding tea to their parents' whisky bottles so they wouldn't notice the missing liquor. One of my daughter's friends stole my arthritis meds out of my bathroom and ended up in the hospital with a stomach bleed from trying to get high on them. She was 13 years old.

At this age, the peer group has more influence than the parent likes to think. The teen is trying to fit in while protesting that they just want to be different. They may wear clothing you don't approve of and hair styles designed to drive you crazy, and you may wonder where your loving child has gone and who this alien creature is.

This is where all the relationship building, structure and family values you have built will sustain you. Decide what you can bend on and what you will not bend on, and stick to it. Confront behaviors you are unwilling to accept at once. Make the consequence fit the behavior if possible. Taking away all phones and computers is huge and should be reserved for major infractions.

Continue to insist on participation in maintaining the home and on family meals. Make your child's friends welcome in your home. This is the best way to monitor behaviors in your own child.

I'd like to talk about time and curfews. Keep it simple and early. There is never a reason for a 13-year-old to be out at midnight, except with a parent at a community event, and you are providing transportation. Know where your child is and whom he or she is with. Know also that your teen will not like it. They will tell you all their friends can stay out, but this is the time to hold the line.

My answer was: I'm not the parent of those kids and it's my responsibility to care for and protect you. When I feel you are ready for more freedom, it will be because I see you being able to handle more responsibility. Until then feel free to use me as your excuse. Say, "My parent is old fashioned and won't let me."

All teens need limits. They may not be strong enough to stand up to peer pressure. You have to stand for them.

Physical activity, music and art should be a part of your teen's life. Kids who are involved in sports do better in school. They are less likely to drink, smoke or do drugs. It also fills the need to be part of a group. However, don't push your child into sports if they have no interest or aptitude for it. Find something else. Being a chess champion is just as valuable as being a football star.

Love your child for who and what he is right now. Accept the teen years for what they are, a time of rapid growth and brain development. It's a time of discovery and a time to build skills for adult living. It's not a straight path. There will be times when it's great fun and times when it's hard. Give them your time, love and discipline as needed. Give them your acceptance.

I had a good friend who constantly asked her child to do things perfectly. She would make her copy her homework over and over until it met her high standards. She was never satisfied with her teen's efforts. The teen left home the day she turned 18 and moved in with a 35-year-old man. It took several years to rebuild the relationship with her mother. The mother was trying to teach her daughter to put forth her best effort. What she really taught was that she could never be good enough to win her mother's approval and that she was unworthy of love. It's sad because I know that mother did love her daughter. She spent years in therapy to rebuild the relationship and they have a good relationship now. The years they lost could have been prevented if the mother had been more accepting of her child and had not expected perfection.

Don't give your child too much, even if you can afford it. Give them the self-esteem that comes from earning it. No 16-year-old should be given a brand new car. They don't have the driving experience to be responsible for it and they will show off to other kids, and may get killed in the process. A teen will take much better care of a car if they had to earn the down payment and if they have to earn their own gas money.

Give them love, your time, and discipline as needed. Give them your acceptance and you will raise a productive adult. Every child has special gifts and they are usually not what we expect. They are usually much, much more, and that is the great joy and blessing of being a parent.

One of the greatest compliments my son ever gave me was telling me how much he learned by being included in the adult parties I had. He said he loved watching how people interacted and how I was able to make people at ease and comfortable in my home. He did not feel left out and he loved it when people would debate current events and tell stories about work. Children do learn social skills by watching others and by watching you. It's important to give them many opportunities to be in social situations that include differing age groups. If they only socialize with other kids, they never learn acceptable adult behaviors.

TV is not a teacher of acceptable behavior, but because there is now so much separation of the generations, it's the only role model a lot of kids have. It's the parent's responsibility to lead by example. Have a party, join a group. Do something with your kids that give them an opportunity to learn what is acceptable. How many young men know how to seat a lady at a table? When is the last time you saw a teen hold a door open for an elderly person? Manners are often the only difference between the person who succeeds and one who never gets the good job.

Language is another thing that should be looked at. Can your teen express himself or herself without using the F word? Count how many times they use it in 30 minutes. Also, count the "you knows" and other bridge words. These are things that make young people look unintelligent and these habits will hurt them as they try to navigate the adult world. Tell your teen that it takes 21 days to form a habit and about 28 days to break a habit. If they are willing to look at changing these behaviors, one way is to fill up a jar with dimes. Every time they use the F word, take a dime out and place it in the "parent" jar. At the end of the time period, the teen gets what is left in the jar. It's a good visual reminder and it will motivate some kids to look at the behavior. Not everyone will buy into this, but it works well for those who do.

One of the things that are often missing in the lives of foster children is a sense of community. Many of these children have been separated from family, church, schools, neighborhoods and friends. It's hard to go forward when you have lost your base from which you grow.

That's why it's so important to keep connections in the lives of foster children. It's also vital in the lives of all children. One of the reasons kids get involved in gangs is to have a sense of belonging. This is a basic need in all of us. We are all tribal in our ancestry. Children separated from their tribe, meaning family and community, are missing a part of their identity. Even bad parents still hold some history that a child will need. It may be medical or social, or just answers to why things happened.

Think how hard it would be to erase all of your family history. No knowledge of grandparents, aunts, cousins, ethnicity. Many native children don't know anything about their tribe. Many kids can't tell you about their ancestry at all.

I often say I'm Irish and Native American. People identify themselves as Polish, German, Irish, English, Hispanic, Pacific Islander, etc. We are referring to where our people came from, and there is a sense of pride in that, even though we may have been descended from people who came to America 200 years ago. We are all Americans, but we still want to know our history. These doors are often closed to foster children, especially if they have grown up in the system and lost contact with birth families.

One of the issues I deal with in the foster home system is racial prejudice. I have had kids from many diverse backgrounds living in my home and they are already indoctrinated with notions about race and ethnicity that they are reacting to.

One child, who was African American, treated Hispanic children in a cold and hateful way. She would accuse them of taking her things and of being dirty. As she got to know the person, she would become less hostile, but it was hard on the new kids as they came into my home. She was not open to looking at her pattern of thinking. She actually developed a strong friendship with a Hispanic girl, who was her roommate, but it took several months, and the Hispanic girl was so open and friendly that it was impossible to resist her charm. I don't think she ever gave up her deep-seated prejudice, even though she was generally not an unkind person.

We try very hard to help children maintain their cultural identity and we do that by having discussions about food and health practices from different cultures and areas of the world. We talk about celebrations, and I ask questions like, "What would your grandmother do when you got sick? What would she cook? What was the most important holiday in your home? Did you go to church? Did you have music in your home? What was that like?" When children tell you about these things, they are connecting with their culture and they feel valued by your interest. You also have a chance to learn things you may not have been exposed to in your life.

I had a child from Cambodia who explained the practice of cupping and coining, which I found very interesting. She said it was very effective for colds and fevers. As best as I could understand the practice, it is a way of bringing blood to the surface of the skin, which cools the body of fevers and stimulates an immune response. That's not so different from the practice of sweating out a fever.

One of the things I would share with the kids was the practice my mother used of putting onion poultices on our chests when we had a bad cold. She would give us a warm bath and cover us with blankets. She would fry several large chopped onions and wrap them in an old towel she kept for that purpose. She would place this on our chest when she determined that it was cool enough to not burn, but warm enough to create soothing heat. The smell of the onions would open up the nasal passages and get the mucus flowing so breathing would become easier, and the next day we always felt better.

She also kept a jar of homemade salve made from mixing pure sulfur and lard. This was used for all cuts and scrapes. We never got a serious infection. Who knows, maybe this would work on some of our superbugs today.

Every culture has some of these home remedies, and it is interesting to see what gets passed down. It's also a way for children to see that they are part of a long line and that they can pass wisdom to their own children when they grow up and become parents. The oral tradition is not dead. It's what holds cultures together.

As I have become old, I find that I think of my mother often, and though she has been dead many years, I remember so many things she did to keep us healthy and to give us a sense of our family history. Much of it had to do with food, and though we like to think modern wisdom is superior, in fact much of what she taught is being rediscovered today. She would say, "Try to make sure your plate has three colors of food on it, green, orange and yellow! Eat less meat and more vegetables. Eat a good breakfast every day. Eat slowly; savor the taste of your food. Fresh from the garden is best."

These are wisdoms from the past. Your foster children may not know them, but you can be their teacher. If they didn't have a wise grandmother or mother, you can take that role. A foster parent is, above all else, a teacher. The secret to teaching is in the living. If you make kale soup the kids like, they will be willing to cook kale when they grow up.

I make a potato medley that the kids love and it is simple to prepare. Simply fry a large onion in olive oil and toss in a yam or sweet potato, a white potato, a blue and gold potato, all cut into bite-size pieces, add salt and lots of black pepper, add about ½ cup of water, cover and cook until the potatoes are soft.

This may be the first time kids have seen yams cooked in a way that is not covered in sugar. Most kids tell me they don't like yams, so I ask them to try two bites, and they are surprised to find they do like them. I let them know they don't have to eat anything they hate, but to at least try them. That way they are more willing to try new things.

Kids today are living in a world we could not have imagined 30 years ago. The need to be connected 24/7 by cell, text and social media is such a new phenomenon that we cannot know the full extent of the changes in behavior, maturity and social functioning that these things may cause.

The need for instant gratification seems to be greater, and I wonder if the lack of quiet time to reflect will cause a rise in impulsive behavior. Will there be an increase in attention deficit disorder? We don't really know. I have seen kids that can't turn off their phones to come to the table and kids who are not getting enough sleep because they can't shut off their phones. I have to wonder what is so important that they become very anxious when they aren't electronically connected.

When I worked at Ryther Drug and Alcohol Treatment Center, the boys were not allowed to have cell phones, and it seemed that some of the boys had more trouble giving up their cell phones than giving up the drugs.

I have no idea how this will affect human behavior long-term. It may be a good thing and will prepare children to live in the new fast paced society, but I still feel that parents need to exercise more control. There should be some tech-free time each day for kids to connect with the real physical world around them. They need to be in touch with their bodies, the natural world, and be aware of other people around them. Creativity is developed in the un-programmed part of our minds. It creates something where nothing existed, and if every waking moment is filled with chatter, there is no space where creativity can flourish.

Once again, the old adage, moderation in all things, makes good sense. I think a good guideline for teens might be no cell phones during family meals, no cell phones after bedtime and no cell phones while riding in the car. Again, that's family time and great conversations happen when you are driving your kids to school, to sporting events or to dental appointments. These are what I call "side by side" conversations because they are less threatening than face-to-face eye contact talks. The parent needs to be unplugged at the same time. Lead by example.

I remember asking my granddaughter, while we were driving somewhere, if she was having sex with her boyfriend. She was surprised by the question and said, "Grandma! Do I have to answer that question?!" I laughed and said, "No, I'm just concerned that you may need birth control and I want to make sure you are protected." We then had a discussion about birth control and the pros and cons of several kinds. She told me she was on the pill and so far it was working well for her. I told her that some antibiotics would make her birth control ineffective and this was new information for her. We had a great discussion and she was not embarrassed because she was not looking at me. She felt respected and it was actually a good bonding experience because she knew I was not being judgmental. I was caring about her welfare. This would not have happened if she or I had been using a cell phone in the car.

Monitor the computer usage and the social media sites your kids use. Make sure they understand that what they put online can be seen by prospective employers, by college admission boards and even the police department. If they are ever involved in a crime, as a victim or perpetrator, social media sites may be used against them. It's serious business. If a young man is "sexting," sending or possessing nude pictures of underage girls, that is a crime and he can be charged as a sex offender. Again, that's serious business and many teens are unaware of the fact that it is a crime. This is another good "car conversation" to have with your teen.

Recognize that most teens are more tech savvy than adults, but we still need to monitor who they are communicating with and what they are posting for the world to see. This is a case of teens not being able to project the future, so they don't realize how serious these things can be.

When a girl sends a nude photo of herself to her boyfriend, she doesn't expect that he will show all his buddies because she is sure that he is the love of her life. But a month later when the relationship is over, he will, because it's the nature of young men to brag, and a girl's reputation can take a serious hit. She may be ridiculed by her peers, and there have been suicides over these kinds of incidents. Many teens don't think these things could ever happen to them, but it's actually very common. That's why, as parents, we must monitor, teach and inform whenever we can.

The pitfalls of Junior High are another area I'd like to touch on. Seventh, eighth and ninth grade can be brutal! This is the age when kids are most vulnerable. Kids get bullied and made to feel like outcasts over the smallest things. The social landscape at school is like walking through a minefield, or a swamp with alligators and water snakes all around. Everyone is trying to fit in and the rules change every day. Girls are mean to each other because they are so insecure about their own ability to fit in. Peer pressure is terrible at this age, and kids will take chances and do stupid things without forethought and forget everything you have tried to teach.

Be super vigilant and notice any changes in behavior, study habits and grades. Also notice if there is a change in friends. These are warning signs of trouble. This is the time to be a nosy parent. Find out what's going on in the life of your child.

It's good to have your child involved in other things besides school at this age. Karate, dance, skating, sports, church groups, all are good to help your child to see themselves as more than who they are in school. It helps to see that the school environment is not all there is.

This is the age where kids get into drugs. Girls get pregnant or have multiple sex partners just to try to find acceptance. They cannot see that it is a time of limited experience. It is their whole life to them. Add to that the problem of hormones, bad skin, being too thin, too fat, too tall, too shy, and every day can become torture.

How can a parent help? Face time! Family time: doing things with your kids and encouraging things outside of school where they can be successful. Volunteering is a good thing at this age. Help is needed at animal shelters, food banks, scouts. The world is full of opportunities, but you as a parent caregiver must seek them out with your child. They are unable to do these things without your help.

Fortunately, this is a time limited experience and usually by tenth grade the teen has begun to focus on learning adult behaviors, like driving, high school sports, getting a job, etc., even if it is only in their minds. They begin to see there is a future beyond high school.

This is also the beginning of the distancing period where they will challenge your ideas, your advice and your control. They begin to see themselves as being separate from the family system, and a parent must begin to honor this as they try to define themselves as young adults. Drugs and alcohol are still the monsters in the closet, and you must continue to watch for signs of abuse. If you think your child is using, don't be afraid to insist on a drug test. This is not hard to do. You can purchase a test or you can use a lab. The labs cost $40 to $75 for a drug screen, depending on what they are testing for. What if you get a positive test? The next step is drug education, then outpatient treatment, then inpatient treatment. Don't wait and hope it will go away. Keep testing, keep monitoring behavior, and continue to love and support your child and help them to see how important their life is.

The only anchor the child has at this time is family. The only thing that will make them think twice is knowing that mom and dad will be disappointed if they make bad choices.

This is where it gets really tricky in parenting other people's children. The lifetime relationship is not there.

One of the things I use is to "foster a dream." All kids have dreams. If you can find out what that dream is, you can make a plan with the child showing a time line and steps needed to reach that goal. Once again, the purpose is to give them something to focus on besides the social environment of school and a way to strengthen their own identity.

Some basic realities of the teen years are: All girls want to be admired and loved; all boys want to have sex and be admired, and be powerful and "cool."

Looks are very important at this age. Go hang out in the school parking lot and see what kids are wearing. Know the school dress code. It is your best friend. I can't tell you how many times I had to say to young ladies, "Sorry, you can't wear that shirt, or that skirt, it doesn't meet the school dress code. They gripe and grumble, but they comply and cover up their nubile bodies rather than advertise their charms for all the world to see.

They don't know the danger. They are just beginning to experience the power of their sexuality and they think flaunting it will get them noticed. It will, but not in a way they know how to handle.

I had a 13-year-old who was walking home from school when a man in a car tried to lure her by holding money out the window and asking her if she needed a ride. I called the police and, as the officer was taking her statement, she said, "Wow! He must have thought I was really hot!"

The officer told her how the Green River killer picked up young girls, killed them and dumped their bodies in the woods, then returned and had sex with their dead bodies until the body decomposed, and then he buried their remains in shallow graves or dumped their remains into the Green River.

She turned pale and got really quiet. He apologized for having to tell her the brutal details, but he wanted her to know the danger she was in.

In the last few years, I have seen a large increase in children with mental illness in the foster care system. Many of them have been placed in my home. Working with these children is very different than working with children who do not have these challenges. There are no books that I know of and no classes on how to parent mentally ill children. One hour of therapy a week for the child does not meet their needs. There is a fine line to be observed about risk, to the child, to the family, and to the neighborhood. I have found that keeping it simple and having a team in place is vital.

Most kids with mental illness need more body space. They often feel threatened and touching them, even in a friendly gesture, can be frightening to them. Do not expect bonding to happen. Give clear directions and move away. Bipolar children cannot bring themselves under control when there is any stimulation. Do not try to reason with them. Make a statement and move away. It may be about school attendance. I say school attendance is required to live in my house. No more discussion. I've made my point. If a child has no audience, they process information more easily. If they have an audience, they escalate.

I try to be polite in my requests. "Please make your bed this morning," then move away. Tell them when they do something well: "Your room looks really good today," "your chore was very well done," etc. This is a positive feedback loop and doesn't give the child a reason to escalate. It also helps them to feel more positive about themselves.

Medications are important for these children and help them to lead functional lives. You may see ritualistic behavior, such as rocking, tapping, humming, etc. This is a way of calming themselves, and I do not interfere with these behaviors. I try to provide a calm environment and let the caseworker and therapist determine case plan, meds, and family involvement. I assess daily if the child is functioning at an acceptable level or if they need a more structured environment like an inpatient setting. If I feel they are slipping, I call in mental health professionals for an evaluation.

There is only so much that can be done in a foster home environment for these children. The group-care facilities that once handled most of these children have been closed. Foster homes are now expected to deal with them. We must stand united in always putting the safety of our families and other children in our care before the needs of mentally ill children. If they are a danger to self or others, they must be placed in a more secure setting.

Mom-

Mom you are the greatest! You took me in your house and took care of me. You gave me advice and comforted me when I was down. You told me to put my head up and be proud. Whenever I had something on my mind, you were there to talk to. When I needed help you were always there to coach me. When I was doing things wrong you told me what was right. You made me feel wanted and warm when I was unwanted and cold. So now I say thank you for being there through all the hard times, because you made my face shine with happiness.

Love, Liz

ON THE NEWS TONIGHT, I SAW A SEGMENT on homeless children in tent camps in Seattle. It is heartbreaking to see this great nation fall so low that we cannot or will not provide shelter for homeless women and children. The temperature will drop to 30 degrees and the wind is blowing at 35 miles per hour. How can we as a nation live with this shame? If we can fight three wars in ten years, we can feed and house our children. If we refuse to see that need, this nation has already become a "third world" country. I have lived my life with the belief that children are our greatest resource. They are the hope of tomorrow and our society's responsibility is to provide for them. If we continue to treat our children as if their lives don't matter, we will raise a generation filled with hate and bitterness in their hearts. They will take this country to task for not providing for them when they were unable to provide for themselves.

To "foster" is to promote wellbeing in another. To foster a child is to provide a safe and loving environment where he can grow and reach his potential. We can all "foster" children in doing whatever we can, so that they aren't sleeping in tents on concrete in freezing weather. This is an issue that needs to be addressed in the legislature, in the cities, in the community and nationally. We have a navy base here that has been decommissioned. There are many buildings standing empty. How hard would it be to set up shelters in these buildings?

In all the years I have run a foster home, I have had help from the community in so many ways. One friend routinely buys socks and drops them off at my house. Another friend brings her daughters' clothes that are in beautiful condition. These are clothes that come from high-end stores where I could never afford to shop for the girls. We sometimes are given tickets to sporting events. This is the community fostering our children. The YMCA programs are wonderful and routinely give scholarships to our kids. Thank you each and every person and organization who helps. You are "fostering" our children.

A 16-year-old girl was placed with me, and the social worker had begun family visits between the teen and her mother, who was a recovering drug addict. She lived in a halfway house where she had her own room and bathroom and the teen was allowed to spend weekends with her mother there.

After several weekend visits, the girl mentioned that there were bedbugs at the facility. About two weeks later, the girl told me she found bedbugs in her bed. When I checked her bed, there were little brown bugs about the size of apple seeds on the mattress. I wanted to scream, but I didn't. I carefully bagged all the linens in plastic bags and washed them in hot water with 2 cups of white vinegar in the water. I sprayed the mattress with bug spray and called several exterminators for estimates. I did some research and found that I had a very large problem. It seems bedbugs are very difficult to get rid of and have become resistant to most pesticides. I checked all the other beds in the house and found two bugs in the room next door.

No company would guarantee that they could get rid of them, but Terminex offered a 90-day guarantee. I found out that the only sure way of getting rid of them was by heating the house to 150 degrees for 4 hours or freezing them below -25 degrees, and that they could live for two years without a blood meal. No insecticide would kill the eggs and they could lie dormant for months and hatch and reproduce.

I hired Terminex to get rid of them. We had to bag and wash and dry all the clothing and linens and curtains in both rooms. The Terminex man advised me to replace the bunk boards on the beds because there was cardboard on them, and he said the bugs laid eggs in cardboard. He froze the mattresses with liquid nitrogen and sprayed every surface inside and out, including dressers, slats on the beds, bed frames, picture frames, window seals, curtain rods, lamps, everything. All the pillows, curtains and linens had to be taken to a commercial laundry and washed and dried. This was very expensive. The exterminator charged $1,400 and three weeks later, I found bugs again. I called the exterminator, he resprayed, and I had to re-wash everything. We had to be out of the house for 4 hours each time he sprayed, and that was a real problem. What do you do with two old cats and a 120 lb. American bull dog when the temperature is 35 degrees outside?

The state reimbursed me for the $1,400, but not for the bunk boards, box springs and laundry expenses. Three months later, I still had bugs and my guarantee had run out. Fortunately, they remained in only the two original rooms. I replaced all the mattresses, took up the carpets, and joked about setting the house on fire as the only sure way to rid my home of the scourge.

My son's friend, who did maintenance work for several youth shelters in Snohomish County, said that he used cedar oil and diatomacious earth, both nontoxic, and had very good success in controlling bedbugs. I paid him $120 to spray my house with cedar oil and diatomacious earth. With a dry-sprayer, he dusted all the rooms, closets, bed frames, baseboards, and everything else. He told me to leave the dust and not vacuum it up for a few days. He sprayed cedar oil all around the perimeters of the rooms and doorways. He explained that the cedar oil did not kill the bugs, but they hated the smell of it and would not cross it to go into other rooms. He told me where to get the dry sprayer and the dust, and advised me to spray once a month to kill any new hatchings.

At a hydroponic grow store, I purchased a 5 lb. bag of food-grade dust for $10.95 and a dry sprayer for $14.95. For the next three months, I did not see a bug. Then I found two bugs, but I think they may have come in on some things that had been stored in the garage. I sprayed the rooms again with the dust, and I will keep spraying once a month. This has been a very expensive operation with having to replace beds, box springs and carpets, so I want to share this inexpensive solution.

Now I have kids wash their clothes with hot water and vinegar when they come into my home. I'm hopeful this will prevent another contamination, but that is one of the risks of taking children into your home. These creatures can be picked up in the finest hotels or even in taxicabs, so we are all at risk of contamination. It's not a subject people talk about because no one wants to admit to having bedbugs.

One of my foster children just left my home and I want to tell her story because she is such a good example of what can happen with the right support.

JoAnn came to me when she was in ninth grade. Her mother was a drug addict, and she had been raised by various relatives. She was one of five children, all of whom ended up in the child welfare system. She had a strong family support system and a grandmother who had done her best to keep the family together. JoAnn was quiet and liked to spend time alone reading. She was polite and respectful, but slow to bond with us because she had a strong family, even though they could not care for her. I knew she needed space and respect, and time. She was barely passing in school because she was skipping a lot of classes.

JoAnn had many strengths, but her greatest one was in being able to form relationships with adults who could help her to reach her goals. She was in Girl Scouts and had a mentor who took a personal interest in helping her. She got involved in the Independent Living Program and learned skills about renting an apartment, getting a job, buying a car, and many other skills that young adults need to know. She had a really skilled social worker who put JoAnn in contact with every program that could help her. She graduated from high school and was picked up by the Foster to 21 Program. She enrolled in college and also took a course in entry level banking skills. She was hired by a local bank. She has her own apartment, her own furniture and, at 21, she is making it as a successful young adult.

Why did JoAnn make it when so few foster kids do? She was determined not to live the life her mother had. She realized she could love her family while choosing a different lifestyle. She understood that she was valued by other people and chose to use them as role models. She had a strong team around her: one social worker for six years; a mentor for six years who is still involved in her life; and one foster placement. In other words, she had consistency and predictability. These are all the things that help children to feel valued and to succeed.

I now have another child in my home that just turned 18. She has been with me 15 months, during which she has had four social workers. She has not yet completed her high school requirements and seems very unsure about what to do for her future. She is drifting without a consistent plan, and I fear that she will leave foster care soon because she doesn't like the rules she has to go by. She has a good work ethic, but is unable to manage her money or to resist her impulse to spend her check on junk and cigarettes. I wish I felt more positive about her future. She is not ready to make it and is refusing to participate in the Independent Living Training, so she will not be eligible for housing assistance and other perks from the program.

I really care about this young woman, and it is painful to see her not following through on school and training that she could get. All I can do is support and encourage, but she has to do the work. Maybe she is one who has to learn the hard way.

Fostering is an awesome responsibility and should not be entered into lightly, because you do have the power to affect the lives of these children in a profound way. They come with learned patterns of behavior that may not be working well for them. They will often try to set up the same patterns in your home. It's all they know and, even if it's dysfunctional, it's familiar. It's how they expect the world to work.

A foster parent must be aware and willing to challenge these behaviors. I try to do it in a non-blaming way. If a child is loud and verbally aggressive, I say in a quiet voice, "We don't talk to each other that way in my house. It's hard to understand your point when you are being loud and it feels disrespectful to me. When you are a little calmer, I'll be able to listen." I then walk away. Usually at that point there will be a response that is meant to bait you into continuing to engage. Silence is golden and it's your best tactic to force the child to use a different skill to get her needs met. This begins teaching a new, more effective, way to communicate.

There is also the game of "up the ante" Sometimes they will use everything they can to get you to respond in a way that proves they were right in how they see the world. Listen for statements that give you a clue: "Everybody leaves me." "You don't care about me." "You're not my parent." "I don't have to listen to you." "Everybody tells lies." "You are just doing this for the money." "You don't know what my life is like so you don't know what I need."

One of my stock answers is "You may be wrong about that, but we discussed what was expected to live in my home and that has not changed. I don't yell and scream at you and I don't allow people to treat me that way. If you want respect, then give respect. If you want people to value you, then you must be willing to care about others. Your life is important, but you still have to follow the rules here and wherever you go after here, if you want to have a good life. You still get to decide, but you must be willing to live with the result of your decision. That's how the world works. Yelling, hitting and destroying property are not acceptable behaviors here or anywhere else, and it's not in your best interest to act that way. You can't control the world; you can control yourself."

When a child makes you angry, they do so to control you. It feels like a position of power to them and it's usually behavior they have seen in their family. It takes a little practice to recognize these behaviors for what they are. It's good to remember that foster kids are often in the system because they come from families that don't have good coping skills, and these are the behaviors they have learned. We teach new behaviors by modeling better behaviors.

"No" is a word you must be comfortable with if you are a foster parent. Set your standards and follow through on what you expect. Every teen, including your own, will try to get you to make exceptions to your rule. There may be rare times when you choose to do so, but in general, get comfortable with "no!" It's not your job to please the child. Your job is to nurture and provide a safe secure environment where they can learn and grow. Your job is to teach life skills that will serve them after they leave your home.

A strong work ethic is very important and no one succeeds in life if they are unwilling to work. Many teens in foster care have not had a very good role model to learn this. Their parent may have been mentally or physically ill, or into illegal activities.

Teaching them to care for their own environment is a good place to start. Tying work to reward is important. Allowances should be earned. If you have the resources, extra jobs around the house can provide a way of earning money for a teen. If you choose to do this, make clear what you expect the job to be and how you expect it to be done. Do not pay for shoddy, incomplete work. Make that clear before work begins. This is what will be expected when they enter the workforce, so you are not doing any favors by letting them do a bad job and get paid for it.

I have a child in my home now who asks to earn money ten minutes before she is ready to leave for an activity. I always say No! I explain to her that I don't pay for jobs that are done poorly and she can't possibly earn anything in ten minutes. Next, she tries to negotiate getting paid early and doing the job when she returns. I say "No, do the work, do it well, and then get paid. That's how the world works." She then starts to whine about not being able to pay for whatever activity she had planned. I tell her she is responsible for planning these things and she needs to figure out ahead of time if she can afford it, or allow time to earn the money to pay for it. This may sound harsh, but it is an important life lesson. "Work for what you want! Pay as you go. You are able to earn money for your labor. No one owes you. Life comes at you hard when you have to provide for yourself. One day you will be required to pay rent and buy food. You have to earn your own way."

That's when I hear, "That's not fair! My friends have parents that give them all kinds of things and they get a huge allowance without having to work." My answer is, "You're right, life is not fair and it never will be.

There will always be people worse off than you and better off than you. Help those you can and work to meet your own needs and you will have a good life! The world doesn't owe you a living. You must earn your way!"

In the state of Washington, children in foster care are eligible for free lunches in school. You have to ask for the form and specify that the child is in foster care. They receive the same lunch card as other students and are not singled out in any way. It usually takes a few days to process, so you should pack a lunch for the first week of school or until you get confirmation that they have been entered into the system. You can also get fees paid for sports, ASB cards and yearbooks through a Tree House referral. Some social workers make these referrals and others have to be reminded. This year, my foster kids got school supplies, backpacks, and some really nice clothes from Tree House. This really helps. The payment for foster care is low and does not cover many of the expenses.

The level system grades how much time you must spend on caring for the child's needs. Most kids with fairly normal behaviors are qualified as level one, which pays less than $18 a day. This is supposed to cover food, clothing, housing, utilities, allowances and personal items. Of course, it does not. Children who have more extreme behaviors and require more supervision or have medical needs that require more monitoring are rated at a higher level. This is meant to compensate for the additional time and expense of caring for them.

When the level system was developed, the foster parent filled out the form, but now we are back to the social worker filling it out and the supervisor approving it. They usually do know the child and the behaviors that we will be dealing with.

If we feel that the behaviors are more extreme, we can ask for a reassessment in six months. This works pretty well and I think most social workers do the best they can in a very complex and difficult job. They are caught between a system with limited resources and children with extreme needs, and foster parents just trying to provide for these children. They must know about all the resources available and also spend many hours each month preparing for court, going to court, and following up to make sure the court orders are carried out. Add to that the mandate that they physically see the child at least once a month and visit in the home with the foster parent.

There aren't enough hours in the month, and they often work overtime or off-the-clock. I remember calling at 10:30 PM to leave a message for a social worker and I was surprised when she picked up the phone. She was still at her office doing paper work. People who do not care about the welfare of children would not do a job that hard.

Transitions in life are always hard and it's hard to see our children leave. We never feel that they are ready when they are sure they are. This is true of our own children. With foster children, the process of leaving can be painful because they have often grown up in a system that has provided basic needs and controlled their lives; it has not provided them with practical skills. Half of the kids will end up homeless in the first year. They have no safety net and though much work has been done to correct this, the foster child still sees it as the state controlling their behavior. One of my kids left today and I sent her on her way with hugs and good wishes, and told her to keep her options open and ask for help if she gets into trouble. She feels she is ready to be independent, and she may be. I hope she makes good choices and that she will do well. Life is our teacher and we each have to walk our own path.

I now have two openings for new kids and the other kids are asking "When will we get someone new?" I told them I had already turned down three kids and I would know when the right one was referred. That led to a discussion of "how do you know and what do you look for?" I explained that I look for someone who will fit well with the kids that are already here and someone who is willing to live in this area and go to school. I look at background and associations, and criminal activity. I won't take a kid who is dealing drugs or gang involved because it puts my other kids at risk of harm. I look at history of physical violence and theft. I try to assess the risk against the safety of the home. It is complex.

They were able to accept my explanation and said they wanted someone who would get along with them. I didn't tell them that I like to take a day or two between kids just to process my own sense of loss as my kids emancipate, but it's true that I often need that time for myself. I pretend that it's about cleaning the room and getting it ready, but that's only a part of it. When I know I have done my best with a child and it's time to release her to the world, I need time to let go also.

One of the nice things about watching my girls emancipate is looking forward to a different relationship as they grow into adults. Over the weekend, I had a call from one of my kids wanting instructions on giving a home perm. She remembered me giving her a perm when she was 14, and now she has a young teen daughter. The circle completes itself, and it has always been so with mothers and daughters. We reach backward for wisdom and we pass it on to the next generation. It holds true with our foster children as well as our birth children.

One of my girls called tonight to tell me about how hard she was working in college to finish her BA in nursing. She told me a lovely story about a children's book that she had read about passing love on. She said she had written an essay about me, how she had used me as her role model, how I had taught her to love herself, and how that had made a huge difference in her life. It doesn't get any better than that!

I have laughed and cried, despaired and hoped, but most of all, I have loved all these many, many children that have been placed in my care. I know my life has counted and been well lived. I hope for many more years and the chance to share it with a few more.

To anyone who might consider being a foster parent, I say it's hard, it's wonderful, it's brutal and it's fun. Your heart will break and you will cry, but you will laugh too, and most of all, you will love. That's really what life is all about.

Battling the Stereotype

A Foster Youth Speaks

I'M SITTING THERE WATCHING *FULL HOUSE*, all relaxed after a long day, and then I get a sudden urge to throw the remote at the television. That catchy Sleep Country, U.S.A. jingle comes on as I see these cute kids. They start talking about how much they miss out on school because they move all the time. Or maybe they're saying how cold they are around the holidays and how much they miss their siblings. *How pathetic can they make me look?* But why would I hate this commercial so much if I'm a part of it? Okay, not literally, but theoretically. I'm a foster child, and yes, I don't have many school supplies or winter clothes; and no, I don't see my family very often at all. Does that really make me pathetic, though? I think not.

Before I was in foster care I had been going to the same school for almost a year. I had my set of friends and I was continuing to make more. I had my place in the school; I was comfortable with who I was and the way in which I belonged to the school. So when I became a foster child and my friends found out, it wasn't a big deal. Everyone already knew me. Now all they had to do was add to that image the fact that I was in foster care. Their perception of me did not change. However, when I moved and had to switch schools for my junior year, things didn't go smoothly.

It was the first week of school and all my teachers had us doing some introduction activity. My English class was no exception. We needed to find three things to represent my family, a hobby, and a community I belong to. After a long debate with myself, I decided to bring a painting for my hobby, and one thing to represent my family and community, which was a matching necklace my sisters and I have. It was tough to open up to people who barely knew my name. Telling them I bought this for my sisters and me because I'm in foster care and we're all split up not only scared me, but them as well. I got this look of awkward terror from the whole room. Foster children aren't commonly stumbled upon, but did they really have to look at me like a zoo exhibit? Since no one in the school had known me before, and I had put myself on display. I unknowingly gave every student in that school a pre-conceived image of me. I'm sure they've all heard about kids in state care; all the street kids that are underprivileged and defiant with no motivation. So the moment I said, "…I'm in foster care," I scribbled all over my picture. They no longer saw me as just the new girl.

Though I have been through stereotypical events that people expect a child in care would go through, I am constantly trying to disprove the stereotype that foster kids are pathetic. I hate this Sleep Country, U.S.A commercial because the statements said in the commercial make foster children sound pitiful and hopeless. I am not hopeless; I take all the negative times I have experienced and learn very positive lessons from them. I don't want sympathy, I want empathy. Foster kids need people in their life, not donated items. As long as we get the support system all other kids have, we will go just as far. I am determined to prove all those who doubt me wrong.

About the Author

LOREITA RICHARDS began her work with children as a Head Start teacher in Mississippi. She worked with the U.S.O. in Puerto Rico where she provided support to young service men and women.

She attended Intra American University where she studied Art and Intra Cultural relations. She is a registered counselor and hypnotherapist. She has spent most of her adult life working with teens. She is a gifted artist and often teaches art to teens. Her wisdom and dedication to this population has given many young people the tools they need to become productive adults.